Craft Furniture
The Legacy of the Human Hand

Craft Furniture
The Legacy of the Human Hand

Schiffer Publishing Ltd®

ower Valley Road, Atglen, PA 19310 USA

Dennis Blankemeyer

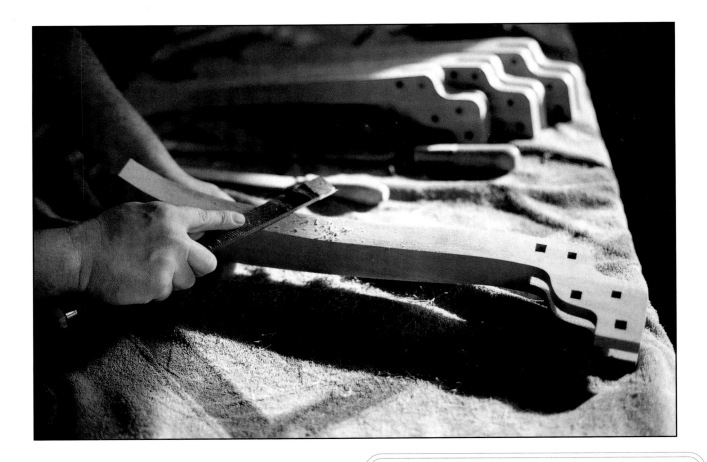

Library of Congress Cataloging-in-Publication Data

Blankemeyer, Dennis.
     Craft furniture : the legacy of the human hand / by
Dennis Blankemeyer.
        p. cm.
     ISBN 0-7643-1787-3 (Hardcover)
1. Furniture making—United States. 2. Cabinetmakers—
United States—Biography. I. Title. TT194.B55 2003
749.213—dc21
                                    2002156071

Designed by John P. Cheek
Type set in Zurich BT/Zurich BT

ISBN: 0-7643-1787-3
Printed in China

Published by Schiffer Publishing Ltd.
4880 Lower Valley Road
Atglen, PA 19310
Phone: (610) 593-1777; Fax: (610) 593-2002
E-mail: Schifferbk@aol.com
Please visit our web site catalog at
www.schifferbooks.com
We are always looking for people to write books
on new and related subjects. If you have an idea
for a book please contact us at the above address.

This book may be purchased from the publisher.
Include $3.95 for shipping.
Please try your bookstore first.
You may write for a free catalog.

In Europe, Schiffer books are distributed by
Bushwood Books
6 Marksbury Ave.
Kew Gardens
Surrey TW9 4JF England
Phone: 44 (0) 20 8392-8585;
Fax: 44 (0) 20 8392-9876
E-mail: Bushwd@aol.com
Free postage in the U.K., Europe; air mail at cost.

Contents

Dedication

To my wife, Denise, and children, Brooke, Jacob, and
Faith. You are a blessing to me each day.

Acknowledgments

First and foremost, I am indebted to Rebecca Bell for her assistance; the input she had in the book was tremendous. Her encouragement, thoroughness, and diligence played an integral part in the writing process.

A heartfelt thank you is also extended to:

Larry Hamill and his assistant Pam Willis of Larry Hamill Photography, whose beautiful photography helped set the tone for the book.

Robert Leonard, Anne Sims, Mansfield Bascom, and Ruth Esherick Bascom of The Wharton Esherick Museum, for taking the time to give me a glimpse of the "Dean of American Craftsmen."

James Krenov, David Welter, and the students and faculty of the College of Redwoods Fine Woodworking program, who create quiet work "with wakened hands."

Sam Maloof, whose warmth and encouragement will always be a true blessing. And to Sam's assistant, Roslyn Bock, who made the trip to the San Gabriel Mountains a very enjoyable experience.

Mira Nakashima Yarnall, your pleasant demeanor and willingness to help came at a time when it was sorely needed.

Brian and Kathy Condran, for your wonderful hospitality on our whirlwind trip to California.

Kassie Rose, for reviewing the early manuscript and giving valued assistance.

Doug Congdon-Martin and Peter Schiffer, who gave me the opportunity to write this book.

All the craftspeople in this book, whose extraordinary talents and love of their craft can hopefully be revealed throughout every page. I hope their stories become a part of your conversations around the coffee table.

And finally to my wife, Denise, whose love and affection is cherished each and every day.

Preface

"The beauty of God is the cause of all the being that is. Thus beauty is an absolute and has to do with recognition."

Eric Gill,
A Holy Tradition of Working

Working for 10 years in various large architectural firms, I expected to design the world the way I thought it should be. Unfortunately, instead of designing the next Empire State Building, I was given the honor of drafting toilet partitions, shuffling paperwork, and producing sheet after sheet of construction drawings for $100 million buildings. I worked day after day in an impersonal cubicle in a perfectly aligned cube farm, envying the old architects and craftsmen who were able to create the masterpieces that our modern society couldn't seem to emulate.

While attending architecture school in Cincinnati, Ohio, I had become aware of the Arts and Crafts and Prairie School Movements. I voraciously read all I could about Frank Lloyd Wright (an unwritten rule for any budding young architect) and admired vases and tiles by Rookwood Pottery, a Cincinnati company that received national recognition during the movement. I was left with the nagging impression that craftsmanship, purity of design, and the harmony of well-designed interiors were from a bygone era.

About that same time, my wife, Denise, and I needed to buy furniture for our Craftsman style home. We began searching for Arts & Crafts antiques, but were quickly dissuaded after discovering the price of those antiques to be in the stratosphere. It seemed our only option was to travel to a big box furniture store. We weren't very excited about the prospect, but felt we had no other alternative.

Walking through the doors of the store, we were overwhelmed by the selection and were disappointed by the quality of craftsmanship and design. So many styles, so little choice. The store was a cluttered maze with chairs stacked on top of dining tables (the impending scratches, I presume, were to give the furniture the distressed look). After opening the door to an armoire and having it practically fall off its hinges, we swiftly left without venturing into the other 40,000 square feet of "luxurious" offerings.

Where is the craftsmanship that we so admire in a one hundred year-old building, in an antique piece of furniture, or in hand-hammered metalwork? Is there anybody creating and building furniture that we could pass on to our grandchildren? With the many choices in our modern society, is factory furniture at the big box retail stores our only option?

I began to ask myself how we can derive any meaning in our lives from the shoddy offerings commonly found. How can one feel at home in an environment of mass-produced items made by machines, where the work and pride of the human hand is all but obsolete? And then I wondered if anyone shared my sentiments.

Impassioned with the notion of finding craftspeople that were producing furniture with the techniques used a hundred years ago, I started my search. While in a bookstore I came across the magazines *Fine Woodworking, Home Furniture* (it has since ceased publication), and *American Bungalow*. In their pages I found my answer: there are many craftspeople producing creative and unconventional furniture unlike any I had ever seen.

Denise and I spent the next few years dreaming of opening a retail store and design studio that would provide the public with an alternative to manufactured furniture and uninspired design. As we thought about it, it became clear that the technologies of the late twentieth century had left a void that many who search for significance in their lives are trying to fill. Gourmet coffee, *real* bread bakeries (none of that wimpy white stuff), microbreweries, and even the popularity of the book *The Not So Big House* by Sarah Susanka, which illustrated the importance of values and simplicity, all seem to be attempts to answer the need for quality in life.

In the twentieth century Americans have grown increasingly more detached from our innate kinship with nature, as we compromise our inner needs to seek instead the contrived styles and passing fads of the day. But as I researched, I confirmed that Americans are not finding contentment in square footage or sport-utility vehicles, but are turning back toward the natural world and its simple pleasures. We endeavor to find a sanctuary from our fast-paced lives, our own corner of the world that makes sense. I firmly believe that those places exhibit qualities of simplicity, nature, and human interaction.

After ten years devoted to craft furniture I felt compelled to write this book. I endeavor to tell the stories of some of the craftspeople who have found peace in working with natural materials and fulfillment in being able to offer something that people use, live with, cherish, and want to hand down to their children.

Throughout this writing experience, my focus has been to seek out those who have chosen to live a simpler life, where dignity and pride are drawn from the results of their labor and excellence is achieved through trial and error and old-fashioned elbow grease. Unfortunately, this book can only include a small sampling of the countless talented craftspeople across the country. Many who love fine woodwork will be dismayed to find that some seminal figures have not been included, luminaries from the first generation such as Arthur Espenet Carpenter, Wendell Castle, Tage Frid, Garry Knox Bennett, Jere Osgood and Bob Stocksdale, and a host of shining stars among contemporary craftspeople, including Wendy Maruyama, Jack Larimore, Tommy Simpson, Judy Kensley McKie. My only response is that I may need to write another book.

The Simple Life

"Simplicity, simplicity!"
Henry David Thoreau

"Make it your ambition to lead a quiet life, to mind your own business, and to work with your hands."
1 Thessalonians 3:11

Photographer: Larry Hamill.

Photographer: Larry Hamill.

Photographer: Larry Hamill.

Handcrafted furniture and simple living have a direct relationship with each other. It's difficult to live with handcrafted furniture without feeling the benefits of slowing down to enjoy it. Admirers of handcrafted furniture are sympathetic to the draw of nature. They understand the value and significance that handcrafted furniture can bring to their lives, offering a glimpse of honesty that makes them feel good to look at it, touch it, and enjoy it. They also recognize the importance of living in the present; consciously and intimately.

Many think that living simply means living in a small, sparsely furnished home with no luxuries. But the reality of simple living is that it allows us to unburden ourselves from clutter and intrusive technology, enabling us to embrace the things that really matter such as family, relationships, community, and spiritual well-being.

Living the simple life can mean many things to many people. It can be as radical as leaving the corporate life and the impersonal skyscraper and moving to a quaint home in the rolling hills of the country. Or, it can be as minor as cutting the hours watching TV, turning the mobile phone off while driving, and taking more walks in the park. In essence it is about living deliberately and fully aware of why you live your life the way you do. Instead of going through life on autopilot or just reacting to one event after another in your life, it is about making conscious decisions that coincide with your ideals.

If there is anything that Americans require, it is simplicity. It has become a mantra that has permeated the country. From magazines and TV to support groups and classes, there is a growing movement to simplify our daily lives by removing clutter, cutting down on superfluous activities, and making informed choices.

The craftspeople represented in this book are among those who have slowed down to pursue the interests and activities that delight them. Jim Probst and his wife Glenda moved to West Virginia during the height of the "back to the land" movement and

Facing Page:
The rich tones of craft furniture provide serenity, in a hectic world.
Photographer: Brad Feinknopf.

literally lived off their patch of land for several years. Brian Boggs fell in love with the idea of felling a tree and then crafting the wood into a chair. John Lomas and Charles Shackleton moved from England and Ireland, respectively, to take part in the rewarding and demanding lifestyle of an American craft furniture maker.

The people making craft furniture explore designs that are expressive of their personality, with craftsmanship that harkens back to another age. Unlike most period furniture, with its elaborate carvings, turned legs, and claw feet, American craft furniture is almost always designed with straightforward, uncomplicated forms. The excellence of this type of handcrafted furniture is in the skill of the joinery, the beauty of the wood grain, and its simplicity of design. Frank Lloyd Wright spoke profoundly when he said, "As we live and as we are, Simplicity – with a capital "S" – is difficult to comprehend nowadays. We are no longer truly simple. We no longer live in simple terms, in simple times or places. Life is a more complex struggle now. It is now valiant to be simple, a courageous thing to even want to be simple. It is a spiritual thing to comprehend what simplicity means."[1]

In craft furniture the joinery is left exposed. Full mortise and tenon joints, precise dovetails, and butterfly inlays are recognized as beautiful forms used as expressive ornament and not merely functional. The wood reveals the work of the Creator, which accentuates the grain pattern. It's this integrity and honesty that gives the craftsperson and their clients the meaning and spiritual comfort we all crave, whether we are aware of it or not. Meaning comes from the craftsperson working purposefully and diligently with their hands to provide permanence and beauty. Comfort comes from the warmth, allure, and the sensuous feel of wood. The work becomes an extension of the craftsperson's philosophy – living the simple life.

Photographer: Larry Hamill.

Photographer: Larry Hamill.

Photographer: Larry Hamill.

Photographer: Larry Hamill.

Photographer: Larry Hamill.

Facing page:
Furniture by craftsman Michael Colca exhibits
the warmth and beauty of handcrafted furniture. Photographer: Andrew Yates.

Photographer: Larry Hamill.

<u>The Simple Life</u>

16

The home as a sanctuary is expressed in the bedroom furniture of Berkeley Mills. Photographer: Sean Sullivan.

The Natural Home

"Nature is the best and only true guide to scale, proportions, and the right relation of parts to the whole and whole to parts."
Frank Lloyd Wright

"High Tech/High Touch"
John Naisbitt, author

High touch. Photographer: Larry Hamill.

Most technological innovations promise greater freedom and more free time, tricking us into believing that we can compress more and more into shorter time frames. But the reality is that our up-to-the-minute lifestyles continue to detach us from nature's cycles and landscapes. We wake up in the morning by the clock radio. The coffeemaker automatically starts. We drive in our climate-controlled vehicle to sit in front of a computer in a sterile office environment. All the while, we are "plugged in" with mobile phones, e-mail, television, Internet, fax machines, and the latest wireless gadgets, which only continue to drive us further away from our innate desire to connect with nature. With this constant intrusion of technology upon our lives, there is a greater need to balance and temper its effects in our lives and in our homes.

Plastic, steel, glass, and rubber are the materials of our wired world, hence most of our sensory experiences originate on a television or computer monitor. Ironically, this *Jetsons'* lifestyle we once found appealing has become a symbol of the cold and impersonal. Is it any wonder that as a society we continue to gravitate and gather together where we receive social interaction? Coffeehouses, malls, local pubs, and the like continue to grow in popularity as we search for significance in our lives and appease our yearnings for social interaction.

In the same way, people are finding beauty and significance in wood furniture and natural materials. They seem to counterbalance the isolation of the wired world with the warmth and comfort of nature. Hand-hammered metals, hand-rubbed wood finishes, and hand-thrown pottery remind us that we are part of the natural world and can use its resources to create the new.

But the balance of our love for nature and our requirements for technology can be a delicate one. It's not quite as simple as buying a television with simulated wood grain. We want the conveniences of technology but don't want to see it. A perfect example is a TV armoire; we bury the TV and our electrical components behind wood, because, quite frankly, a TV is ugly.

If cheapness, speed, and uniformity are the tools for our rapidly changing modern society, then harmony, comfort, and significance provide the necessary ingredients for creating meaning and a sense of place for the home, the workplace, and the community.

High tech. Photographer: Larry Hamill.

High touch. Photographer: Larry Hamill.

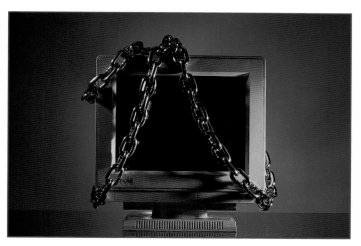

High tech. Photographer: Larry Hamill.

Technology represents:	Nature represents:
Universal	*One-of-a kind*
Plastic & Synthetic	*Warmth of Wood and the Natural*
The Jetsons	*The Andy Griffith Show*
Corporate	*Residential*
Office Building	*Home*
Geometric	*Organic*
Reduction of the Sensory	*Expansion of the Sensory*
Planned Obsolescence	*Craftsmanship*
FedEx	*The Corner Bakery*
Global Village	*Neighborhood*
Skyscraper	*Intimate Scale*

Stopping technology from developing and becoming more complex is not the answer. We cannot undiscover computers, wireless communications, or the television. We can, however, adapt and adjust to the technologies and be wary of their consequences.

In the 1950s and 1960s plastic and metal furniture was *en vogue* as America was about to blast off into a brave new world. Craftsmanship was thought by many to be merely a relic of the past. Instead, disposable furniture and planned obsolescence was the order of the day.

Recently, we have renewed our interest in handcrafted items. Quilts, folk art, hand-blown glass, pottery, and handcrafted furniture are responses to our human need to have something with meaning in our sterile and antiseptic age. Each piece of handcrafted furniture has its own unique story, involving the craftsperson who made it, the inspiration for the piece, the materials used, and its final realization.

The popularity of the minimalist interior with the shiny chrome surfaces is dead; it was a fad. We long for links to our past and to honest values such as community, church, and family. Straightforward looks and natural materials that are honest, rugged, and refined have been, and dare I say will always be, the means by which humans are comforted. We now know that, if we are going to live with technology increasingly infused into our daily lives, we need to have balance. It starts with unpretentiousness, honesty, and integrity in our personal values as well as our surroundings.

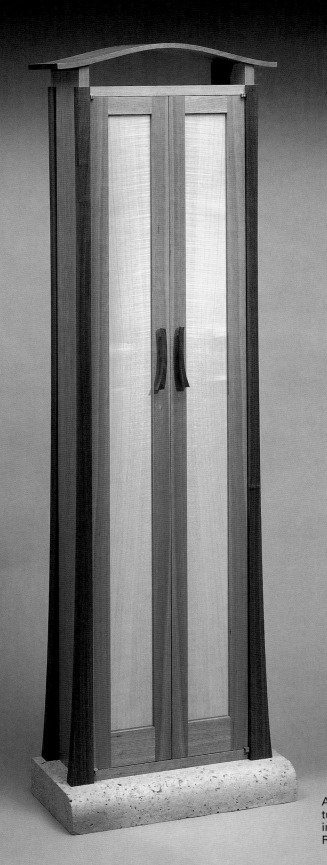

A CD cabinet by Raymond Bock turns a much needed container into a work of art. Photographer: Raymond Bock.

High touch. Photographer: Larry Hamill.

High tech. Photographer: Larry Hamill.

High touch.
Photographer:
Larry Hamill.

High tech.
Photographer:
Larry Hamill.

The Natural Home

The office tansu by Gene Agress of Berkeley Mills conceals the requirements of a home office behind an attractive facade. Photographer: Sean Sullivan.

Photographer: Larry Hamill.

High tech.
Photographer: Larry Hamill.

High touch.
Photographer: Larry Hamill.

High tech.
Photographer: Larry Hamill.

<u>The Natural Home</u>

An audio cabinet by Thomas Stangeland hides the stereo components behind a veil of wood. Photographer: Greg Krogstad.

Audio cabinet — open.
Photographer: Greg Krogstad.

Craftsmanship

"The workmanship of risk and the workmanship of certainty."
David Pye,
The Nature and
Art of Workmanship

"The special quality of beauty in crafts is that it is a beauty of intimacy. Since the articles are to be lived with every day, this quality of intimacy is a natural requirement. Such beauty establishes a world of grace and feeling."
Sõetsu Yanagi,
The Unknown Craftsman

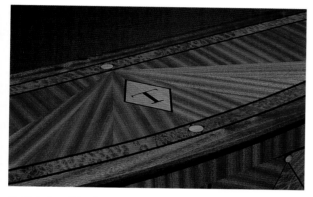

Buffet detail by Lorna Secrest of Works of Wood. Photographer: Lorna Secrest.

Hand-planing at Charles Shackleton's workshop. Photographer: Thomas Ames Jr.

Madison Avenue uses the term *handcrafted* as a clever and profitable marketing tool to sell what are often shoddy goods. The advertisers are confident that by using such a term they will draw upon the emotional needs of their consumers. *Handcrafted* conjures up images of care, detail, and passion while *factory* denotes antiseptic and synthetic processes. Unfortunately, handcrafted has been so excessively used these days that the description has become watered down and ubiquitous.

Webster's New World Dictionary describes *handcraft* "to make by hand with craftsmanship." The term clearly describes work that involves the use of the human hand, but these days, it is used to sell just about anything. Billion dollar beer companies such as Budweiser advertise, "Handcrafted at a brewery near you," and multimillion dollar furniture manufacturers promote their furniture as handcrafted, complete with a gray-haired "craftsman" with chisel in hand and wood shavings at his feet. According to the corporate world's broad definitions, someone picking a piece of furniture off an assembly line would warrant the designation *handcrafted.* These companies know that when purchasing a gift for someone, the buyer is never excited to hear about the process of the assembly line, but is interested to hear about the person crafting an object just for them. We are tired of the mass goods produced in factories, whether it is furniture or food, and we are romanced by the idea of the individual craftsperson creating honest goods.

Craft furniture is truly made by hand; it demonstrates the care and passion that a furniture maker commits to his or her craft. It is the alternative to the mass produced "fine" furniture, antiques, and traditional reproductions.

The difference involves all aspects of creating and making a piece of furniture. From the initial inspiration, to the meticulous wood selection, the precise joinery, and the alluring finish. All of

Bench detail by Daniel Kagay of White Wind Woodworking. Photographer: Ron Whitfield.

this combined with superior workmanship, passion, and the intimacy of the work distinguishes it from other furniture. Only when all of these elements are lovingly composed can we call furniture *handcrafted*.

Although in both craft furniture and art furniture the designer and craftsperson are one, they are not to be confused. Art furniture by definition is not functional. It is usually highly expressive of the personality of the artist and is often whimsical. In contrast craft furniture is as functional as it is beautiful, every element has a purpose, and it's made to be used and enjoyed. Craft furniture merges art (beauty) and architecture (function). Craft furniture is more than aesthetically pleasing to the eye. It entails design and solid construction details that are appreciated by the avid collector and the casual observer.

The Hand and the Machine

The majority of the craftspeople presented in this book use a combination of handwork and machinery. Machinery is used to take the drudgery and monotony out of tasks; it becomes just another tool like the chisel and the plane. It does not, however, become the focal point of the construction process. Handwork is used to accentuate the human connection and provide the bond between the wood, the craftsperson, and the admirer.

Just as one needs balance between nature and technology, it is also of great importance to delicately balance handwork and machinery. The language of the factory, where the machine is used for the *replacement* of the body, is cheaper, faster, and more convenient. The language of the individual furniture maker, where the machine is used only as an *extension* of the body, is excellence, worth, and value.

Design

The major furniture companies boast a stale and recycled line of furniture that is designed for planned obsolescence. They operate on a one-size-fits-all strategy. The furniture is mass-produced without the love and care that comes from the heart and hand of an individual.

Craft furniture makers demonstrate an incredible range of originality, uniqueness, and painstaking execution. The furniture and designs are created in the mind of the craftsperson, not contrived from the latest fads or trends of the day. The designs are an expression of the craftsperson's personality, and become the first step in the journey for the designer/craftsman. A small furniture shop typically has its own furniture collections and preferences, but often works with a client to fill a particular need.

Customization is one of the main benefits of working with an independent furniture maker. The craftsman will create a piece made to fulfill one's specific desires. As a result, a client will receive a piece of furniture that will be in harmony with his/her needs, lifestyle, and interior.

Harmony, Order, and Proportion

"There is music wherever there is harmony, order, and proportion."

Sir Thomas Brown

A craftsperson has many questions to consider regarding the need for harmony, order, and proportion. Careful attention to the smallest of details must be taken throughout the furniture building process. For example: how wide should the leg be? Does the piece look too heavy? How will structural considerations affect the design? Many questions must be answered and all the subtle details considered.

Facing Page:
Inlay detail by David B. Hellman and Associates. Photographer: Dean Powell.

Wood Selection

Wood selection is one of the crucial aspects of creating an exquisite piece of furniture. A craftsperson carefully examines each piece of wood so that there will be consistency throughout. They are also able to select the most highly figured wood for the most visible areas, such as tabletops, drawer fronts, and chair arms. In this way each piece of furniture acquires its own unique character and personality. In craft furniture the craftspeople select premium hardwoods with fine grain patterns and color. Wide thick boards are used instead of laminated pieces that have been built up from a number of small pieces glued together.

In furniture factories the crucial task of wood selection employs the least skilled and most poorly paid person on the assembly line. Wood with different grain characteristics and boards from the heart of the tree (heartwood) and edge of the tree (sapwood) are placed together, producing a result that is far from pleasing to the eye. For example, a cherry table with a natural finish can have a disturbing zebra striped appearance because the sapwood and heartwood display an uneven color. One way furniture factories solve this problem is to put a dark stain on the furniture. While this disguises the problem of wood selection, it also conceals the inherent beauty of the grain.

Another main component of wood selection is the use of wood approved by an organization that promotes sustainability of our hardwoods, such as the Forest Stewardship Council, Sustainable Forestry Initiative, American Tree Farm System, Smart Wood, or others. Their marks assure that the tree was harvested responsibly. Many of the craftspeople listed in this book are advocates and members of these organizations.

Joinery

An individual furniture maker uses time-tested joinery techniques, such as the mortise and tenon and dovetail joints. The expressive nature and ornament of craft furniture is in its joinery. The mortise and tenon joint is the strongest joint in furniture making; it allows for expansion and contraction of the wood. When two pieces of wood are joined, the tenon (which is attached to the stretcher) is fitted into the mortise. The dovetail joint is used primarily in drawer construction and is used to join two pieces of wood together. It is so named because it resembles the tail of a dove. Although usually hidden behind the drawer face, a crisp dovetail joint is one of the easiest ways to distinguish handcrafted furniture.

Manufacturers use a tremendous number of nails, pocket screws, pins, and dowels in the construction of their furniture. This makes every connection very weak, and severely reduces the life of the piece.

Overlay vs. Inset

A deception used by the large manufacturers is to make doors and drawers in an overlay style.

In this style the drawer edges cover the opening of the frame. This technique is used to hide shoddy craftsmanship. One can make the drawers without much concern about accuracy, because the drawer face hides the irregular opening. The overlay style is commonly used for kitchen cabinets, not exquisite furniture.

Conversely, inset doors and drawers are used when the frame and the drawers are flush. An inset style is not only more pleasing to the eye, it displays a meticulous attention to detail. The drawers should open and close effortlessly with an even gap around the drawer, and a smooth finish should be expected both inside and out.

Another common aspect of handcrafted furniture that is rarely seen in manufactured furniture is the process of book-matching. This is when a board is split in two and then opened to show a mirror image. The boards are placed next to each other to emphasize the matching grain pattern. This is a time-consuming process, but well worth it in the end.

The Finish

The final step in the furniture process is the finish. The key to this step is the fine sanding. Although it can be a tedious and time-consuming part of the furniture making process, it plays a crucial role concerning the human touch. Most craftspeople do not take pleasure in sanding. It's grimy and dusty work with a certain amount of monotony. But the furniture makers realize that sanding is something that cannot be rushed, and the piece will fail if it isn't pleasing to the touch.

Chair detail by Brian Boggs Chairmakers.
Photographer: Geoff Carr.

China cabinet detail by Arnold
d'Epagnier of Mission Evolution.
Photographer: Michael Latil.

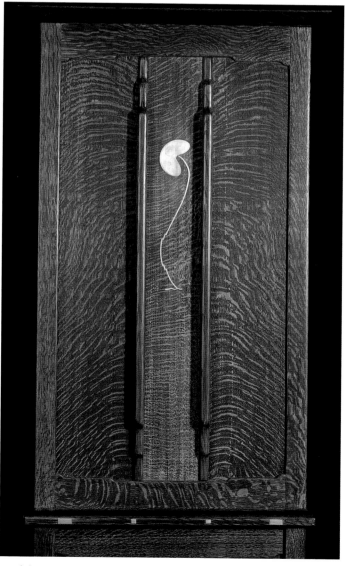

After the sanding is complete, the craftsperson puts on the first coat of finish. It is at this stage that the piece of furniture can first be seen in its full glory. The culmination of all of the craftsperson's hard work, imagination, and elbow grease is when the finish penetrates into the wood, illuminating the grain. "This is always an exciting time in the shop when you get to see for the first time the full effect of the wood choice," explains craftsman Michael Colca.

In the last 50 years we have been misled into thinking a high gloss finish is a distinguishing characteristic of fine furniture, when, in fact, it usually disguises poorly sanded pieces and mismatched boards. Because it is not economical for factories to spend a lot of time sanding, they will provide the minimal amount possible. After being nominally sanded, the furniture is commonly sprayed with coat upon coat of lacquer or polyurethane. When wood is lightly sanded, stained dark, and coated with a high-build finish, the pleasure of touching the actual wood is gone. Instead, you feel a synthetic, perfectly polished top coat.

Costs

Furniture that lasts for a few years and doesn't bring delight is the most expensive furniture one can buy. The prices for craft furniture are very competitive with the fine furniture market. Especially considering it will last 100-200 years. Once the cost is amortized, it is clear that it is a solid investment, and well worth the wait. After all, a "fine" European sports car will typically only last 15-20 years.

The craftsmanship in today's craft furniture can be better than that in some of the world's finest antiques at a fraction of the cost. Early American pieces can sell for over $1 million, while even the top craftsperson's work rarely approach six figures. If the cost of furniture is in proportion to the workmanship that goes into it, then handcrafted furniture is woefully underpriced. In addition, it is a better use of the world's natural materials because the furniture can be passed down to children and grandchildren.

Where to Find It

Many of the craftspeople listed in this book have a website, brochure, or catalog of their work. Also, the Internet has become another increasingly powerful tool for locating talented craftspeople. The Philadelphia Fine Furniture and Furnishings Show, the Fine Furnishings Providence Show, and the American Craft Council Shows are just a few of the many events that exhibit a vast array of styles and furniture makers from across the country.

The recent revitalization of American craft has meant an increased presence in retail stores and galleries.

The Furniture Society is an organization dedicated to promoting the furniture makers and the galleries that show their work. The Furniture Society's mission is: To advance the art of furniture making, by inspiring creativity, promoting excellence, and fostering an understanding of this art and its place in society. They have an excellent website and brochure that list all of its members.

In addition, publishers such as Cambium Press, Schiffer Publishing, and Taunton Press (the folks who also publish *Fine Woodworking*) have devoted many books to the individuals involved in handcrafted furniture.

Nightstand detail by John Lomas of Cotswold Furniture Makers. Photographer: Sean Randall.

Trestle dining table detail by Michael Colca Furniture Maker. Photographer: Andrew Yates.

Chair detail by Berkeley Mills. Photographer: Sean Sullivan.

Desk detail by Brian M. Condran Fine Woodworking. Photographer: Kathleen Bellesiles.

Server detail by Kevin Rodel of Mack & Rodel Studio. Photographer: Dennis Griggs.

Dining set detail by Kevin Kopil Furniture Design.
Photographer: Becky Stayner.

The First Generation

Wharton Esherick, James Krenov, Sam Maloof, and George Nakashima form the foundation on which all contemporary American craft furniture makers stand today. They have had a profound impact and influence on the second generation woodworkers in both furniture design and construction. Through writing, teaching, and single-minded focus, each man has left an indelible mark on the modern revival of craftsmanship.

Wharton Esherick and George Nakashima (now both deceased) had their workshops less than 30 miles from each other outside of Philadelphia, Pennsylvania. Nakashima Woodworks is located in New Hope amongst the rolling hills and bucolic setting of Bucks County. The workshop is now run by Nakashima's daughter Mira and continues to thrive. Esherick's studio and residence is located in Paoli next to scenic Valley Forge National Historical Park. It is now the Wharton Esherick Museum. Unfortunately due to their differing philosophies, Esherick and Nakashima did not correspond with each other.

James Krenov and Sam Maloof call California home. Krenov is located in Fort Bragg, three-and-one-half hours north of San Francisco, and Maloof is located 30 miles east of Los Angeles. The 80-plus-year-old craftsmen are still very active. Both work tremendous hours and are still making furniture. Like Esherick and Nakashima, because of their differing philosophies and personalities, the two men are not friends.

The men came to furniture making from disparate backgrounds and professions: Esherick the frustrated artist, Krenov the boat builder, Maloof the graphic designer, and Nakashima the architect.

They epitomize the designer/craftsman philosophy, and their work expresses their personalities and individual beliefs. They were able to find a market for their work through sheer will and love for the craft.

Photographer: Larry Hamill.

These four individuals have laid the groundwork for the increasing number of amateur and professional woodworkers in America. Their philosophies, works, teachings, and writings are an inspiration and a beacon for furniture makers of all skill levels who wish to achieve some sense of joy through the power of creating, using their mind, body, and spirit.

Wharton Esherick

Wharton Esherick (1887-1970)

Wharton Esherick is not a household name because he eschewed the limelight. He lived a spartan existence in the area known as the Great Valley, just a short walk from Valley Forge National Historical Park. He did not teach students, write books, or travel the country espousing his view on his work. He would simply say, "If you want to know me, look at my work." Born in 1887, Wharton's long and prolific life inspires many craftspeople because of his consummate dedication to his vision.

The home and studio where Wharton spent the majority of his life resemble disparate objects that have been discreetly grouped together, to make a living, breathing entity that reflects the man's ingenious spirit. The building is devoid of the usual quaint historical references, and it does not command a triumphant presence. Instead, it looks as if it had sprouted from the ground, and, like a chameleon, merged with the mature trees of its surroundings. It functions much like a piece of fine cabinetry, with no detail too small to escape Wharton's rapt

Exterior view of home and studio. Photographer: Author

attention. Wharton seems to have formed a prehistoric bond to the landscape and had the insatiable desire to create and influence the world around him.

Inside, each piece of furniture and sculpture has a story. For instance, on his famous three-legged stools, Wharton used wooden hammer handles to make the legs. He had been looking for a use for the hammer handles after purchasing a barrelful. Another chair sits in a corner with its arms and legs made out of wagon wheels.

Everything in his house served the purpose of being both beautiful and functional. The pull cords on light fixtures have small wooden sculptural elements attached at the ends, coat hooks are wooden caricatures of Wharton's assistants, and an elephant tusk becomes a handrail. Even the door hardware is intricately carved out of wood.

Wharton's compulsion to draw and create began early. "He was always drawing, from the time he could hold a pencil," says his daughter Ruth Esherick Bascom. "All his life, he had a pencil and paper in hand. If he didn't have one with him when he would leave home, he would remember it when he got back and start drawing."

Wharton's life was a journey of styles and vocations; he was involved in painting, wood block printing, sculpting, and furniture making. Against his parents' wishes Wharton shunned a life in the business world and enrolled in the Philadelphia School of Fine Arts and two years later entered Pennsylvania Academy of Fine Arts. He eventually grew frustrated with the academic training, finding it difficult to hone his own painting style and voice. Demonstrating his independence and self-reliance, Wharton quit just weeks before graduation and started working in Philadelphia.

After marrying Letticia (Letty) Nofer in 1912, he moved to a farmhouse in Paoli outside of Philadelphia. Wharton spent his time painting and searching for his style. In 1919,

Exterior view of garage and workshop. Photographer: Author

Wharton Esherick

Wharton was invited to teach at an artist colony in Fairhope, Alabama. It was in Fairhope that Wharton met and became lifelong friends with the great American author Sherwood Anderson, who wrote *Winesburg, Ohio*. A year later, Wharton and Letty moved back to Paoli. It was there that Wharton began to use carving tools that Sherwood had given him to carve wood frames for his paintings.

Still focusing on painting, Wharton held his own art shows. To spread the word, he would send out wood block print invitations of his own design. But his invitations and picture frames received more attention than his actual paintings. Giving it one more try, he left for New York City with paintings in hand. He went from gallery to gallery looking for a place to show his work. Unfortunately, Wharton was stymied at every corner. Defeated, he returned to Paoli and never picked up his paintbrushes again. He poured his passions into creating wood sculptures, interiors, furniture, and wood block prints.

Interior of home and studio.

His daughter Ruth recalls him working long hours. "He worked all the time. I didn't think very much of it at the time. Whatever he was doing, he was working," she says. "He kept very regular hours. Started at 9:00 a.m. and sometimes didn't finish until late in the evening." He often had one or two employees who would do the final sanding, but Wharton did all the designing. Even though Wharton worked primarily with his hands, he didn't shun the machine, "Wharton embraced the machine from the beginning. He even made an early band saw out of bicycle wheels," says Ruth.

Wharton felt an intimacy for his work that was imbued in every detail. He did not have to create his objects through another man's eyes, hands, and abilities, but, as the craftsman, he could take his vision wherever he wanted. Wharton's life work continues to be a beacon for craftspeople who wish to live a life doing what they love, a life that cannot be measured by monetary gain.

Interior of dining area.

Solomon Had a Vineyard woodblock print (1927).

Rhythms woodblock print (1922).

January woodblock print (1923).

<u>Wharton Esherick</u>

Oblivion, wooden sculpture from walnut.
Photographer: Author.

Handcarved utensils. Photographer: Author.

<u>Wharton Esherick</u>
43

Telephone alcove. Photographer: Author.

Spiral stair, perhaps Wharton's most famous work, ascends to the second floor.

Photographer: Author.

Wharton Esherick

James Krenov

James Krenov (b. 1920).
Photographer: David Welter.

James Krenov is a dichotomy. While often highly opionated, James has a deep well of sensitivity. His speech is sprinkled with heavy doses of dry wit and sarcasm as he dogmatically explains his stance on furniture making. Until recently he worked and taught in the understated building of the Fine Woodworking program at the College of Redwoods. A reflection of the man, the school he founded is serene, focused, and expressive. It is located in the small town of Fort Bragg (3-1/2 hours north of San Francisco) off beautiful Highway One and next to Northern California's craggy coastline. Now retired from teaching, his story is one of perseverance and unbending conviction.

James was born in Siberia, Russia, in 1920. As a result of the Russian Revolution, his aristocratic parents were sent to Siberia to start a school for the Chukchi people near the Arctic Circle. The living conditions were severe but the area was pristine, and, though harsh, he says that it "was undoubtedly the happiest period of (my) mother's long and unusual life."[1]

The understated building of the Fine Woodworking Program of the College of Redwoods. Photographer: David Welter.

After leaving the Arctic Circle, when James was still a young boy, the family moved frequently, going from Russia to China to the United States and to Canada. They finally settled in Seattle, Washington, where his parents separated, and James and his mother lived in a small cottage on the coast. It was in Seattle that James began to build boats. He and his young friends would often go sailing, but James preferred to sail alone.

After living in Seattle for 10 years, he started working in the nearby shipyards taking care of yachts that were built in the Scandinavian countries of Denmark, Sweden, and Norway. The splendor and craftsmanship of these sleek vessels had a powerful allure. Not long after World War II, at the age of 27, James left America and traveled to Stockholm, Sweden.

In Sweden, James found work in a factory, but it did not take him long to discern that he needed to escape the gloomy, frenetic pace of that kind of work. On the streets of Sweden, he happened upon a store selling well-made furniture. Fortuitously, it was the store of the famed Scandinavian furniture designer Carl Malmsten. James recalls in *A Cabinetmaker's Notebook,* "I met the old man…He wasn't sure that I would be allowed to enter his school, but the thought of having a few foreigners there appealed to him, more as a touch of additional color, as a decoration perhaps, than as a sign of his confidence in them." [2]

During his apprenticeship with Carl Malmsten, James received an overall view of sound construction principles and techniques. It was a progression from his boat building years and another stepping stone toward his growing passion to express himself in his work. After leaving Carl's workshop in 1955, James worked for Malmsten's son making architectural models before setting up his own shop in Bromma, a suburb of Stockholm.

By 1976 James had written his first book, *A Cabinetmaker's Notebook*. In it James poured out his innermost feelings and emotions on woodworking – but it was not your typical how-to woodworking book. James's unpretentious writing style and his description of his own struggles, sacrifices, and spiritual rewards resonated with many aspiring woodworkers. "The book is a confession of failure; it's about someone so stubborn he wouldn't give up," James deadpans.

In the book James described his outlook on life, "I think that what I would like to do before it is too late is to get this across to a few craftsmen-to-be who will work after me, and also to a public which will be there to receive them, because we are living in a time when, I believe, this is important. Fine things in wood are important, not only aesthetically, as oddities or rarities, but because we are becoming aware of the fact that much of life is spent buying and discarding, and buying again, things that are not good. Some of us long to have at least something, somewhere, which will give us harmony and a sense of durability — I won't say permanence, but durability — things that, through the years, become more and more beautiful, things we can leave to our children."[3]

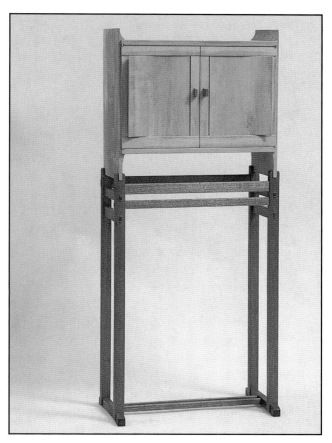

Cabinet on a stand. Wood: pear wood, mahogany stand. Photographer: David Welter.

Throughout the late 1960s and 1970s James accepted various opportunities to teach in the United States. In 1981 he was asked to start a woodworking program for the College of Redwoods. James accepted and became director and founder of the Fine Woodworking program. It's a relatively inexpensive community college and he felt very strongly that all students, regardless of their economic condition should have a chance to learn. He liked the location as well, and says, "I got hooked, along with the salmon, and on a clear day I can I see all the way to Japan."

"The school is unique and works for people of a certain nature, they work long hours, but can take a break and go to the beach," says James. The school teaches virtually no design, but instead teaches sensitivity and the intimate relationship between human and material. Because of the de-emphasis of design, the process can be a struggle. "Teaching in this kind of environment, you have to keep your intolerance to yourself," James says. "We are not restrictive in our ideas, but we shy away from the gaudy and grotesque, we want diversity without conflict."

In his own work, for the last 15 years he has concentrated on "cabinets on a stand." James is realizing the Japanese ideal of doing one thing and doing it to the point of perfection. In

Detail. Photographer: David Welter.

Japan an artist may paint only one species of bird throughout his career. A furniture apprentice may sweep floors for years before he is allowed to take the next step in the craft. Throughout his long career James usually produces only a few large pieces a year.

James continues to write and has published *The Fine Art of Cabinetmaking* (1977), *The Impractical Cabinetmaker* (1979), *James Krenov, Worker in Wood* (1981), and, recently, a compendium titled *With Wakened Hands: Furniture by James Krenov and Students* (2000). Through his strongly held convictions, humor, writing, and teaching, a generation of woodworkers have been influenced by James's call for working quietly and producing quiet work.

Now at the twilight of his career James paints a picture of one who has lived a life of love, love for his work and love for his wife Britta. "We are very fortunate. My wife and I are 80 and 81, and we have been married 51 years. She is an intense and busy lady. Best of all," James says, "she keeps me out of jail."

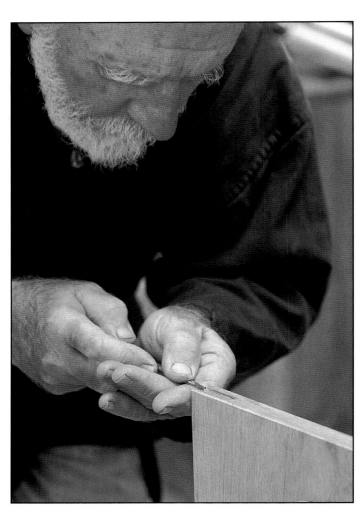

James working. Photographer: David Welter.

James's incomparably subtle detailing. Photographer: David Welter.

Detail. Photographer: David Welter.

Cabinet on a stand. Wood: claro walnut.
Photographer: David Welter.

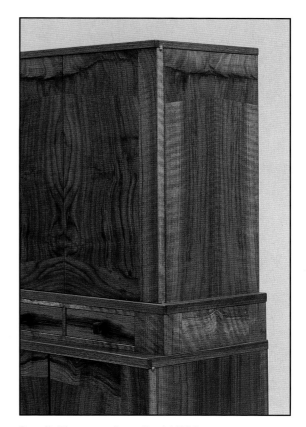

Detail. Photographer: David Welter.

Sam Maloof

Dissatisfied with the two-dimensional world of graphic design, Sam Maloof left his day job to become a full-time woodworker in 1949 at the age of 34. With the constant and ardent love from his now deceased wife, Freda, Sam was able to overcome obstacles, trials, and the unknown to become one of America's most endearing craftsmen.

Now more than 50 years later and recently remarried, Sam is still a busy man. He is filled with Herculean energy at the age of 86. He continues to build approximately 50 pieces of furniture a year with the help of three apprentices. Looking back at a remarkable career, he has an extensive list of museum collections, exhibits, and awards. Most notably, Sam received the John D. and Catherine T. MacArthur Foundation "genius" award, making him the only furniture maker to ever be awarded the honor, had a 65-piece retrospective in the Smithsonian American Art Museum (making it one of the best attended shows in the history of the museum's Renwick Gallery), and is the only living craftsman to contribute to the White House furniture collection.

Sam Maloof (b. 1916). Photographer: Wally Cunningham.

Sam Maloof's masterful design of the quintessential American piece of furniture, the rocker. Wood: walnut. Photographer: Wally Cunningham.

The day my wife and I made the trip to the foot of the San Gabriel Mountains, the workshop and surrounding grounds were a beehive of activity. Two of Maloof's assistants, Mike Johnson and Larry White, were busy in the workshop; Brad Nelson, a craftsman, was visiting for the week; Gere Cavanaugh was reviewing pieces for a Sam Maloof show at a new museum in Beverly Hills; and a man was cleaning windows.

In spite of the hustle and bustle surrounding him, Sam graciously took a large part of the morning to sit down and enchant us with a glimpse into the life of one of America's greatest craftsman. A man with no enemies, he makes everyone feel comfortable. He told me he wished I could have met his first wife, and related to me what she meant to him, "So many good things have happened in my life I just thank God I learned so much from my wife." He said he still pinches himself because he can hardly believe all that has happened.

His home is in the foothills beneath the majestic San Gabriel Mountains in Alta Loma, less than ten miles from his birthplace of Chino, California. Sam's residence has now become a historic landmark. When a freeway was scheduled to be routed through his property, Sam was declared by the California State Legislature as a "Living Legend of California." The state was required to dismantle his home and shop and move it to a new site, just miles from its original location among the lemon groves. His original home now stands as a museum and cultural center dedicated to the arts. A new residence for Sam and his wife was built on the new property.

Born to Lebanese parents in 1916, he was the seventh of nine children. Growing up, young Sam enjoyed drawing and carving intricate toys out of wood. His infectious personality and talent caused two high school teachers to take special note of him. The teachers encouraged him to pursue advanced classes while giving him autonomy to work on his own projects. In fact, he got his first job in graphic design after winning a poster contest that his teacher persuaded him to enter.

After finishing high school Sam found work as a graphic designer until he was drafted into the United States Army in 1941. Because he was always cartooning their unit's mascot, his artistic ability was noticed. He was moved to the battalion office where he produced detailed engineering drawings for gun emplacements. He was quickly promoted from private to master sergeant, making him one of the youngest sergeants in the Army, at age 27.

It wasn't until after he was released from the Army that Sam found his true calling. He became a studio assistant to Millard Sheets who was an accomplished painter, teacher, and architect. Millard's philosophy held that art is part of everyday life and not just something to admire. His influence had a profound effect on Sam's ideas, teaching him new aesthetic possibilities and preparing him to work in different media. Since the days with Millard, Sam has incorporated those ideals into his own life and always tries to pass on the importance of learning about the different forms of art.

Today, Sam is still teaching and still learning. Although he is nationally recognized, Sam feels he hasn't really perfected his style yet. He is known for his broad and deep repertoire of furniture, but perhaps his greatest legacy will be his take on the quintessential American piece of furniture — the humble rocker. With no set sizes or jigs, he uses his own body to measure each rocker. He has received many compliments on the rockers' comfort. It never seems to matter if a person is six feet or five feet tall, each rocker feels like it was made just for him or

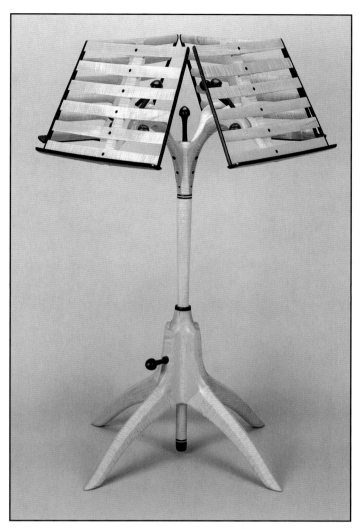

Quartet music stand. Wood: maple, ebony, purpleheart. Photographer: Gene Sasse.

her. Each unique rocker has a sumptuous finish that begs to be caressed and sat in. My wife Denise described sitting in a Maloof rocker as "melting away." (It was probably even more comfortable to her because she was seven months pregnant and had five days of hard travel preceding our visit.) Sam's clients may wait years for a rocker, and each one commands a rather hefty sum.

Sam is still deeply involved in the making of his furniture. He feels strongly that the designer and craftsperson be one and the same. "For me it is not enough to be a designer only," he says in his book, *Sam Maloof Woodworker*. "I want to be able to work as I please, to change a piece of wood into an object that contributes something beautiful and useful to life…to be able to work as we please is a God-given privilege."[1]

Sam treats each chair with extreme care from beginning to end. When he selects boards, he says, "I depend entirely on my experience, my instinct, my intuition, my heart, and my eye. I do not select with my head. The choices come from my gut, not from between my ears."[2] He continues to design and assemble each piece, while his assistants help sand and finish. Reviewing each piece after they leave for the day, Sam takes careful notes. He records subtle changes that may require additional hours of laborious sanding. This close observance is just one example of the intimacy and passion Sam feels for his work. Sam says, "I don't sell through shops; clients call me and I work one on one. Nothing leaves the shop that I haven't designed and put together. I deal with the clients myself and develop friendships. I like to know who I am working for, and never advertise." Sam explains that he only recently made business cards because he "got tired of writing everything out all the time."

His clients number in the thousands and he views them all as friends, often visiting their homes. "I don't think I have a client that I have not become very good friends with," Sam admits. "The only problem is that you don't like to charge them what you have to charge them."

Dining set. Wood: walnut. Photographer: Sam Maloof.

Sam with President Jimmy Carter. Photographer: Alfreda Maloof.

Freestanding cradle. Wood: walnut. Photographer: Gene Sasse.

Low-back chair. Wood: walnut. Photographer: Gene Sasse.

Sam Maloof

Nakashima Woodworkers

Mira Nakashima-Yarnall's diminutive frame may be a bit deceiving. Although small in stature she is not small in presence. Mira is a strong woman maintaining and continuing a tradition. With the weight of her father's legacy upon her shoulders she proceeds with grace and competence. It has been ten years since her father, George Nakashima, passed away, but Nakashima Woodworkers is still thriving in New Hope, Pennsylvania.

It is indistinguishable whether it is her friendly and accommodating demeanor or her strength and intelligence that strikes you initially. There is an intense conviction in her that drives her to continue a mission she did not create, yet sustains today. Her competence is embodied in her knowledgeable expertise. From knowing the details of the mundane menial tasks to overseeing the large tables and chairs being produced, one thing is certain: Nakashima Woodworkers is in good hands.

George Nakashima (1905-1990) and Mira Nakashima-Yarnall (b. 1942). Portrait by William A. Smith. Photographer: Robert Hunsicker.

Touring the grounds with Mira is a delightful experience. Only open to visitors on Saturdays, the grounds are quiet, serene, and unremarkable. Low-lying redwood brown buildings fleck the shaded hillside. There is a faint sound of sawing in the distance, birds singing in the trees, and the crunch of leaves underfoot. A peaceful quiet is attached to the entire expanse. As Mira visits each building, one where the chairs are assembled, another the showroom, and another a barn chocked full of wood, she greets each employee and her sentiment is warmly reciprocated. The workers are few, but highly skilled, helpful, and knowledgeable. They exhibit a sense of casual comfort only attainable when one is at ease with one's handwork and employer.

The barns overflow with various wood species from all over the world, the results of many trips both she and her father have made in search of timber. Walking about the grounds she said that additional barns were built to house the growing number of cut logs. Sometimes a log will sit in the barn 10 years before finding its ultimate destiny. Mira, too, is passionate about making sure the tree and its prospective owners are right for each other. Her father explained

The Minguren Museum located on the Nakashima property in New Hope, Pennsylvania. Photographer: Robert Hunsicker.

the significance of this process in his book, *The Soul of a Tree*, writing that in board selection, "There must be a union between the spirit in wood and the spirit in man."[1]

Such details allure people from across the globe to Nakashima Woodworkers. From traveling the world to look for lumber, to selecting the appropriate boards for each unique owner, to the intricate details of discovering the tree's ultimate destiny and bringing it into fruition, craft furniture is an undertaking that Mira learned from her father George.

By family obligation or simply love for the craft, Mira's life is Nakashima Woodworkers. Her story begins in an internment camp in Idaho during the Second World War. When she was still a small child, the family ventured to eastern Pennsylvania, where her father and mother began the business. After earning a degree in architecture from Harvard and later a master's from Waseda University in Tokyo, Mira returned to New Hope. She began her work as a secretary in the company, while continuing to learn more about the business, especially the design aspects. After her father suffered a stroke in 1989, Mira took on more responsibilities and secured the business. A year later, George passed away and Mira was faced with her biggest challenge yet. With a backlog of orders three years in the making, many people believed there was no Nakashima Woodworkers without George. Nearly half the orders were cancelled, and anxiety grew. The lean years didn't last long, as people began to realize that Mira had been the backbone of the business for quite some time.

Creating beauty, not art, is how George described the process of turning lumber into exquisite tables and chairs. Finding the beauty in a tree and showcasing it was a skill that he was not only able to master, but also to pass on to his eldest child. Although both of their styles exhibit the same ideals, they are uniquely different. Mira's line is called "Keisho," which means "continuation." It is a bit more "spaceship-like" as her young son once observed. George's designs are a combination of the simplicity of both Japanese and Shaker styles.

George Nakashima was no ordinary man. His passion for life and its cycles was great, instilling in him an insight that others seemed to lack. He was so in love and in tune with nature and trees that he could envision the future of a tree. He could see through its outer layer and into its soul. He explains in his book, "A tree is perhaps our most intimate contact with nature; each tree has its own particular destiny, its own special yearning to be fulfilled."[2]

Minguren II dining table and *Conoid* chairs. Wood: claro walnut.

Tsuitate spatial room divider. Wood: claro walnut. Photographer: Robert Hunsicker.

Nakashima Woodworkers

These ideals did not come effortlessly. His devotion developed through years of study and observation. George began his life in the Pacific Northwest. Born in 1905 with an innate affinity for nature, he voraciously explored the mountains, woods, trees, and ponds around his home. After studying architecture at the University of Washington, he went on to graduate studies at Massachusetts Institute of Technology, and later at New York College. Before long, he embarked on a vagabond trip around the world that lasted seven years.

Michener coffee table. Wood: claro walnut. Photographer: Robert Hunsicker.

His kinship with the trees, which began in his native Washington, grew stronger when he saw the twelve hundred year-old keyaki in Japan. His adoration of the tree grew into a lifelong passion, a true longing for the pursuit and discovery of the final destiny of a tree. His journeys throughout the world exposed him to other cultures' beliefs and the near universal respect for nature. The influence this had on him was profound. "It is an art and a soul satisfying adventure to walk through the forests of the world," he explains, "to commune with trees and be in harmony with nature."[3]

While in Tokyo he stayed in his maternal grandmother's home and become acquainted with Japanese carpentry methods. He grew attached to these methods and used them in his designs. Upon returning

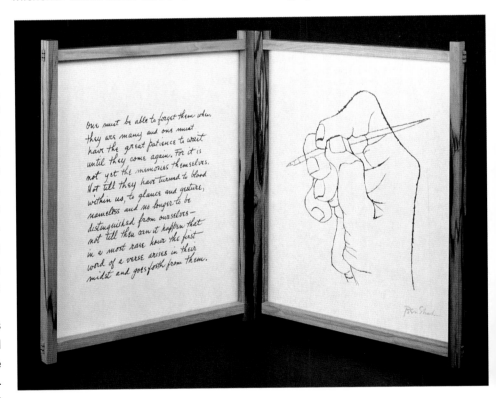

Picture frame for Ben Shahn prints. Photographer: George Erml.

to the United States, his enchantment with architecture dissolved after observing the mediocre craftsmanship used in the execution of so-called great architecture. He turned to woodworking instead, enabling him to be in control of the whole process from beginning to end. Just after choosing his occupation and setting up shop in Seattle, he was sent to an internment camp in Idaho during the Second World War. This was not a likely place for career development, but it was there that he met a Japanese carpenter who instilled in him the necessary skills for the perfection of his craft. In George's book, *The Soul of a Tree*, he says, "Working with him was a rewarding experience and one that I have greatly appreciated."[4] The carpenter taught him both design and craftsmanship.

Once the family was allowed to move east, when Mira was still only a small child, they headed to a friend's farm in eastern Pennsylvania. From meager beginnings, George, his wife Marion, daughter Mira, and, later, son Kevin established Nakashima Woodworkers.

It was the personal interaction that made the business special. George desired to discover the true destiny of the tree, execute that, and allow the wood to speak. Releasing the tree's natural beauty, mindful labor and respect for nature, and making sure to "work with nature, not violate it" are all part, George believed, of bringing out the "soul of a tree" and allowing it to continue in a different but still beautiful form.

George's work is internationally known. It has been exhibited in some of the world's most prestigious institutions including the New York Metropolitan Museum, the Boston Museum of Fine Arts, the Victoria and Albert Museum in London, and the National Museum of Modern Art in Tokyo. Mira is an active proponent of teaching about her father's work and lectures frequently.

Mira is also continuing her father's dream to place peace altars on at least five continents. The most recent one was placed in Moscow in May 1999. It commemorated the fiftieth anniversary of the United Nations. The first one was placed at the Cathedral of St. John the Divine in New York City and the second one in Auroville, India. Mira carries on her father's sentiments, "that through the gifting of concrete symbols of peace—tables formed by nature aspiring to the Divine, worked by human hands and consecrated to peace—universal, peace may some day permeate the entire globe."[5]

Lectern. Wood: cherry. Photographer: Chris Santarella.

Simon coffee table. Wood: figured bubinga, cherry. Photographer: Robert Hunsicker.

Nakashima Woodworkers

Greenrock side table. Wood: English walnut, American walnut. Photographer: Robert Hunsicker.

The Second Generation

"America is the only land in the whole earth wherein a dream like this may be realized; for here alone tradition is without shackles, and the soul of man free to grow, to mature, to seek its own."

Louis Sullivan,
Kindergarten Chats

"There is probably never going to be much room in the market for meticulous, costly, one-of-a-kind furniture sold through art galleries. At another level, there may be a place for the designer/craftsman/entrepreneur who can design well (which may mean fashionably), manage a shop full of assistants, and be a skillful salesman and businessman operating his own urban showroom. Are there such Chippendales in our future?"

A. U. Chastain-Chapman in
Contemporary American Woodworkers

Each furniture maker has a unique story. One may have begun as an architect, chef, glassblower, or teacher, but somewhere along the way a divergent path was chosen, a path that rejected the corporate malaise for the ebb and flow of a livelihood connected with nature. The craftspeople represented in this book embody the independent spirit that throughout history has been a symbol of Americans. These iconoclasts have forged an identity and expression as varied as beautiful oak trees in a forest.

The second generation furniture makers gave up a steady salary, benefits, certainty, and pensions, but in return they were granted something that cannot be bought – independence, independence to build their own designs and the freedom to create. They create furniture that is inspiring and uplifting that pours out of their heart, head, and hand.

The furniture in this book may look similar and seem to have uniformity, but on closer inspection subtle differences are revealed. There are variations in form, expression, and an individual use of pattern, color, and light.

The independent furniture maker struggles with many questions that impact his/her relationship with the work. For instance, he/she must choose whether to hire assistants and risk compromising the work or work alone. He/she must make decisions about what wood species to use and the ethics of using exotic woods. The craftsperson must find the right balance of machine and handwork, and they must also keep in mind proportion, function, harmony, and balance, while refining ideas and techniques.

Each craftsperson answers the questions differently and in his or her own way. Some attest to the importance of being the sole contributor on the journey from inspiration to completion. Others feel that education is the conduit to continuing the craftsmanship. But at the end of the day, it does not matter if one works alone or in a shop of twenty assistants or whether they use veneers, exotic woods, or machines. Instead, the question that must be answered confidently is – does the work reflect ideals of integrity, honesty, and love? If yes, then God and man applaud.

Cotswold Furniture Makers

"When we build, let us think that we build forever. Let it not be for present delight, nor for present use alone; let it be such work as our descendants will thank us for, and let us think, as we lay stone on stone, that a time is to come when those stones will be held sacred because our hands have touched them, and that men will say as they look upon the labour and wrought substance of them, See! this our fathers did for us."

John Ruskin,
The Seven Lamps
of Architecture

In the heart of the English countryside in the nineteenth century, among the stone cottages and rolling hills, a new movement was formed. In the quaint villages of the Cotswolds a quiet revolution took place. As the Arts and Crafts movement grew, ornate English Victorian design and the cheaply made furnishings produced in factories were rejected and replaced with a reverence for beauty and simplicity, and new designs that reflected these ideals. Sidney Barnsley, Edward Barnsley, and Ernest Gimson were the prominent figures of this designer/craftsman philosophy that became known as the Cotswold School. They believed the Cotswolds to be a utopia that should serve as a model for the rest of England. In contrast to the dingy living conditions of the streets of London that many of the masses were subjected to, the country life and its principles were considered favorable to the quality of life. This movement turned into a philosophy of living and working.

Almost a century later, John Lomas moved to the Cotswolds to immerse himself in its ideals and history after first being inspired at the

John Lomas (b. 1958). Photographer: Randall Perry.

London College of Furniture and West Dean College where he attended. John had no desire to become "a corporate nobody" and decided to create his own legacy. He chose the creative and inspiring life of a furniture maker. Shortly after moving there, he opened Hunt & Lomas, a conservation and restoration furniture workshop, which is still in existence today.

Ironically, John had a physical connection with one of his heroes, Ernest Gimson. While visiting an auction in the Cotswolds, he purchased a set of tools. After a little research, he discovered the former owner of the set was an apprentice to Peter van der Waals, who was the foreman for

Photographer: Sean Randall.

Gimson. After Gimson's death, many of the employees continued to work under van der Waals at his new shop. John has the pleasure to use these very same tools in the furniture he makes today.

John moved to America in 1992 and embarked on another side of furniture making, the meticulous work of recreating 18th century antiques. In the shop of Bretschneider & Associates, John could take as long as three months to build one piece of furniture due to the intense handwork, carvings, and moldings. It was this unique experience, combined with the ideals he learned while in the Cotswolds, that formed the basis for his own lines of furniture. The synthesis of the 18th century classical proportion and the clean lines of the Cotswold School can be seen in his current designs. John describes it as "an attention to quality and detail that strives for perfection."

Two short years after moving to the States, John opened Cotswold Furniture Makers. Now his home is nestled in the foothills of the Green Mountains, just south of Middlebury, Vermont. It is not unlike the charming English countryside. A former dairy barn was restored and converted into his workshop. He now employs four skilled craftsmen and one apprentice to carry out his designs and construction philosophy.

When discussing that philosophy, John explains, "I have three main design goals: First, I endeavor to create useful furniture that is pleasing to the touch and gentle on the eye. Second, I try to design each piece to fit harmoniously into any setting without dominating it. Finally, I want the owners of our furniture to experience pleasure in its use for as long as they live."

John has not forgotten where he first became captivated with the skill of furniture making. In tribute to the region that gave birth to a lifelong passion, each piece of furniture is signed by the craftsman and then embossed with a unique Cotswold logo. The logo is a squirrel holding an oak branch. It was taken from a 1904 Ernest Gimson design that was found originally on a pair of andirons. John had it reproduced in pewter to be inlaid discretely into every piece. The squirrel, he says, is to "signify a lifetime of pleasure and use that can be expected from each piece."

John's picturesque workshop near the Green Mountains. Photographer: Randall Perry.

Regency sideboard. Wood: cherry, ebonized pulls. Photographer: Sean Randall.

Left:
Sapperton bed detail. Photographer: Sean Randall.

Below:
Sapperton spindle bed. Wood: quartersawn white oak.
Photographer: Sean Randall.

Cotswold Furniture Makers

Right:
Gloucester dining table detail. Photographer: Sean Randall.

Below:
Gloucester dining table. Wood: cherry, walnut detailing. Chair seats: leather. Photographer: Sean Randall.

<u>Cotswold Furniture Makers</u>

Fox Brothers
Furniture Studio

"Mixing furniture styles, accessories, and art can be a bold statement of individuality. The same goes for original art and one-of-a-kind furniture."

John Naisbitt, *Megatrends*
(client of Fox Brothers
Furniture Studio)

For Henry Fox of Fox Brothers Furniture Studio, furniture making came about as an accident. In his first years out of college, he began coaching the crew rowing team of Trinity College (his alma mater). After four short years of coaching and building boats on the side, he decided that coaching would not be his lifetime vocation. Refocusing on his long-held interest in architecture and building, he turned to a friend who made furniture. This led to a long series of "accidental occurrences," as he puts it, to implement the title of furniture maker.

Actually, creating and crafting with wood was nothing new to Henry. He remembers that as a small boy of eight he built three boats of his own design. "One of them floated," he admits sheepishly. He improved upon his skills and continued to build and repair rowing shells, which he refers to as "floating furniture 60 feet long."

Henry S. Fox (b. 1958). Photographer: Author.

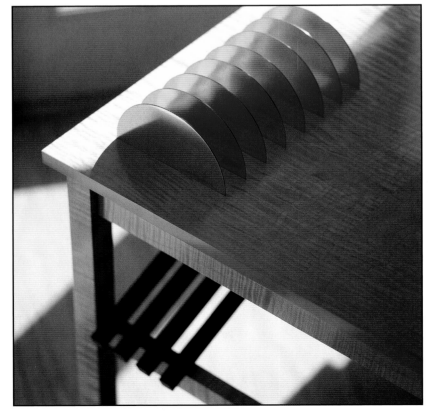

Photographer: Eric Roth.

Now concentrating his passions on th world of furniture making, his designs hav been described as sleek and minimalistic. Th influences of Henry's rowing experience wit its emphasis on aerodynamics are obviou in his work. The furniture also exhibits uniqu combinations of materials, featuring divers wood combinations and the merging of ma terials like steel, copper leaf, and stone.

Because most of his work is commis sioned, he keeps the needs and wants of th client in mind while he weaves together th aspects of form, function, and comfort. On thing that is always apparent is his ability t create a statement of individuality with eac piece.

Krongard cabinet. Wood: curly cherry veneer, wenge, maple. Trim: gold leaf, paint. Photographer: Bill Truslow.

Fox Brothers Furniture Studio

Henry's furniture may be contemporary, but his inspiration lies in an age-old virtue: love for his two sons (William & Orren) and his wife Libby. In fact, even the name Fox Brothers Furniture Studio refers to his two young sons. Most of his furniture designs, in one way or another, are a reflection of his family. Many of his ideas are conceived during precious family moments now preserved in the physical form of a chair, table, or chest. Henry explains that he is also motivated through original thought, materials, and simplicity, which he describes as the "bedrock" of his style.

He works in a former auto dealership; the showroom is located in the front of the building, and the

02 chair. Wood: tiger maple. Metal: stainless steel. Chair seat: fabric. Photographer: Bill Truslow.

workshop is in back. Henry designs all the furniture and works with his assistants on the construction of each piece. Using automobiles as a metaphor, Henry compares his workshop to building custom cars, and the large furniture manufacturers to General Motors or Ford.

Among Henry's many accolades is his ability to be chosen year after year in the prestigious exhibition and sale of contemporary crafts at the Smithsonian Craft Show. He is often one of 120 artisans chosen out of over 16,000 applicants from around the country. The show takes place at the National Building Museum in Washington D.C. every April.

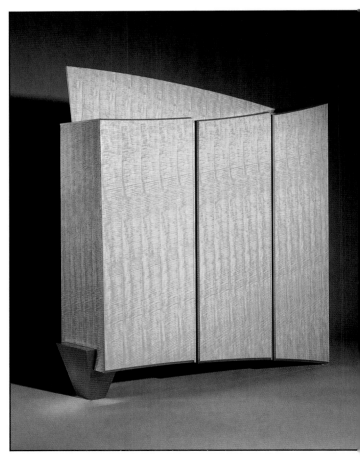

Happy Jumbo armoire. Wood: anigre, ebony. Metal: bronze. Photographer: Bill Truslow.

Fox Brothers Furniture Studio

Zero chair. Wood: ebonized cherry, ash. Chair seat and back: Dacron.
Photographer: Bill Truslow.

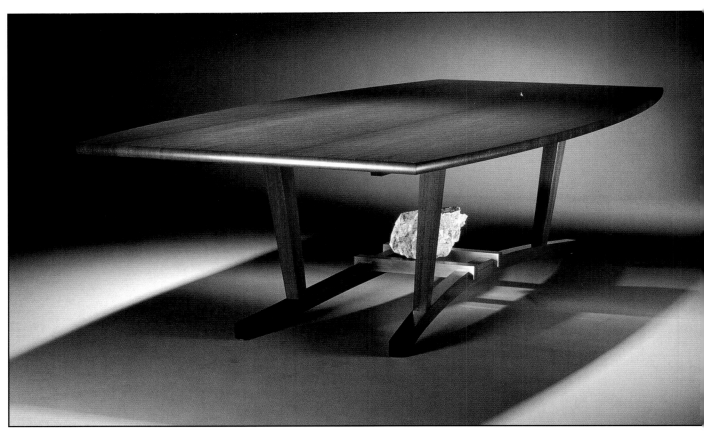

Egret dining table. Wood: wenge. Base detail: bronze, stone. Photographer: Bill Truslow.

Luna bed. Wood: Swiss pear, tiger maple, ebony. Photographer: Bill Truslow.

<u>Fox Brothers Furniture Studio</u>

Blaise Gaston, Inc.

"There are painters who transform the sun into a yellow spot,
but there are others who, thanks to their art and intelligence,
transform a yellow spot into the sun."

Pablo Picasso

Fluidity and movement are the two things that come to mind when one looks upon Blaise Gaston's furniture. He is able to emulate the way in which organic structures (whether human, animal, or plant) grow. Each piece combines grace and functionality. He is moved by nature and it is apparent in every chair, table, and case piece. They look as if they could get up and walk away, or like they have just sprouted from the ground on which they stand. Most importantly, they are always functional, for Blaise feels strongly that each piece needs to be functional, move the spirit, and be impeccably made.

He has been making impeccable furniture since he was six years old. Well, maybe it wasn't quite perfect then, but it was a dollhouse that he and his mom made for his sister. By the time he was eight he had shown so much interest in furniture making that his father made him a workbench (a gift that his father complains about to this day because of the consequent calluses).

For Christmas of his ninth year Blaise was given furniture making lessons during which he remembers making a steering wheel for his go-cart. It is not surprising that by the time he reached the eighth grade he wanted to take a wood shop class. His teachers were against it, due to the fact he was on the "college track," and told him that if he took shop he wouldn't be accepted into a good college. After a quick call from his father (a history professor at the University of Virginia), Blaise became the only student at the school who didn't have to take World History so he could study shop.

The experience did not keep Blaise from entering a good college. Four years later, he was admitted into one of the best furniture design schools in the country, the School of American Crafts at Rochester Institute of Technology. While studying there, he was inspired by his teacher Jere Osgood (a nationally known craftsman), who had a way of bringing design to life. He also learned many lessons on what NOT to do. The first time he used a joiner, Blaise took the guard off because the board was five inches and the joiner was only four. And, as he puts it, "the ends of two fingers were sewn back on soon thereafter." Another early lesson came when Blaise first replaced a saw blade

Blaise Gaston (b. 1953). Photographer: Philip Beaurline.

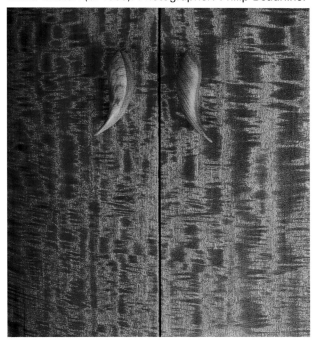

Photographer: Philip Beaurline.

Wall Unit. Wood: sapele pomele, mahogany. Paint: iridescent blue. Photographer: Philip Beaurline.

Blaise Gaston, Inc.

...le. Wood: walnut. Photographer: Philip Beaurline.

and managed to rip a very large oak board in half through a constant plume of smoke. He had put the blade on backwards.

After moving back to his hometown of Charlottesville, Virginia, he began to make pieces with "both sensibility and passion." Blaise describes his pieces as ranging from fanciful to formal, with the highest quality of craftsmanship. The influences of nature are evident in most of his pieces. He maintains that his inspiration comes from animals, trees, or the curve of a woman's leg (most especially his wife's). The organic lines follow the flank of a deer or wing of a bird. "The forms come to life," Blaise says, "through carving, lamination, and traditional joinery." His sculptural elements serve as decoration and structure. A recent addition to his repertoire is the unexpected use of color; he uses it for light and to draw the eye.

...ng table. Wood: bubinga. Photographer: Philip Beaurline.

Dining table detail. Photographer: Philip Beaurline.

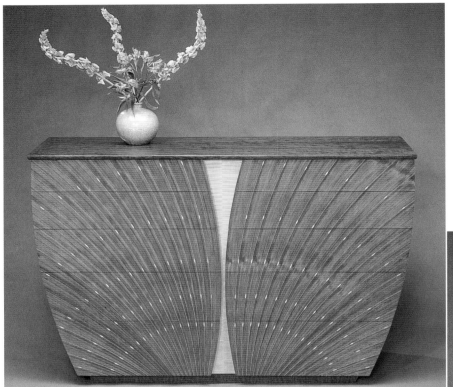

Cabinet. Wood: bubinga. Inlay: curly maple. Photographer: Alan Housel.

Dining chair. Wood: walnut. Photographer: Philip Beaurline.

Blaise Gaston, Inc.

David B. Hellman
and Associates

"The whole construction was carefully thought out, and there was a reason for every detail. The idea was to eliminate everything unnecessary, to make the whole as direct and simple as possible, but always with the beautiful in mind."
Henry Greene

Everyone has a first love, and for David Hellman it was the distinctive designs of Charles and Henry Mather Greene, California's most famous architects of the Craftsman style home. From the one-of-a-kind grandeur of their distinctive homes and interiors to the craftsmanship that was executed by the Hall brothers, David found inspiration for his work and has never looked back.

Whether it's an exact reproduction or an adaptation, it is all in the Greene & Greene vocabulary for David. Many years ago when he discovered their work, he found he was enraptured by the Greene's attention to detail and design aesthetic and in awe of the "high degree of accomplished cabinetmaking" executed by the craftsmen employed by Peter and John Hall. In 1989 David opened his own workshop that would strive to match those extremely high standards of craftsmanship. Taking notes from those who have gone before, he builds each piece with care and thoughtfulness, from design to finish.

The Greenes' work is still visible today in the many "ultimate bungalows" scattered throughout Pasadena, California. After attending school in one of the first manual training schools in America, Charles and Henry Greene decided to stay in California after a visit to their parents. They established a practice and, by 1907, were attracting wealthy clients. The Greenes believed in incorporating the architecture, furnishings, and landscape into a cohesive whole. Their designs strayed away from the heavy, straightforward designs of their peers (Frank Lloyd Wright, Gustav Stickley, etc.), in favor of softer, subtler detailing. One of their first commissions was the Blacker House, a 12,000 square foot home with oriental accents. In the living room of this home was the distinctive mahogany and ebony armchair that David superbly reconstructs today.

David B. Hellman (b. 1958). Photographer: Author.

Photographer: Dean Powell.

Signature rocker. Wood: mahogany, ebony accents. Seat: leather.
Photographer: Dean Powell.

Maintaining that the chair is the most challenging type of furniture to create, David proclaims, "This chair has served as a magnet for people, drawing them in to run their fingers over the raised and carved inlay of silver, oak, and purple heart." Subtle curves and gentle stepping where one part meets another are what makes each piece pleasing also to the eye.

The chair is a complexity in design. David describes it best by elaborating, "The front leg undulates into the arm, and the back posts move out and back as they widen and twist into the top rail." The carvings on the legs and back are all hand executed, and the ebony accents are raised and softened. The carvings at the bottom of all four legs cause the chair to raise off the floor. This is an interpretation of Chinese decoration known as "lift," which is simply described as a "linear abstraction of a cloud form."[1] The top rail has an ornate and complicated sweep that involves tedious hand sculpting on thick mahogany. Every detail is reproduced down to the hand-tied coil springs in the cushion.

No doubt, David is passionate about the furniture he creates. The structure of each piece becomes the decorative element. "Where two different parts meet," says David, "it is highlighted and becomes a celebration of joinery."

Thorsen house sideboard. Wood: mahogany, ebony accents. Inlay: oak, walnut, abalone.
Photographer: Dean Powell.

<u>David B. Hellman and Associates</u>

77

Leather arm chairs. Wood: mahogany, ebony. Chair seat and back: leather.
Photographer: Lance Patterson.

Blacker arm chairs. Wood: mahogany, ebony accents, raised and carved inlay.
Chair seat: fabric. Photographer: Lance Patterson.

<u>David B. Hellman and Associates</u>

78

Gamble table. Wood: mahogany, ebony accents. Photographer: Lance Patterson.

Kevin Kopil
Furniture Design

"Form follows function – that has been misunderstood. Form
and function should be one, joined in a spiritual union."
Frank Lloyd Wright

Creating furniture as an independent craftsperson is not an easy job. Of course, neither is designing furniture or running two retail stores, for that matter, but Kevin Kopil manages quite nicely. It takes incredible drive and energy to produce furniture and own your own retail establishments. Surely, some things are sacrificed? "I have so many designs in my head," says Kevin, "I wish the only thing that I had to do is build furniture, but it's the thing I do least of all." Fortunately, he is able to generate a few new designs each year.

Kevin has been working with wood since he was ten years old. Although he pursued higher education in the field of electronics, after graduation he took a job as an apprentice in an architectural woodworking shop instead. By the time he was age 24 he had moved to Vermont (where he resides today) and began woodworking full time. Just six years later, he opened his own furniture studio where he creates furniture with five assistants.

Kevin Kopil (b. 1958). Photographer: Becky Stayner.

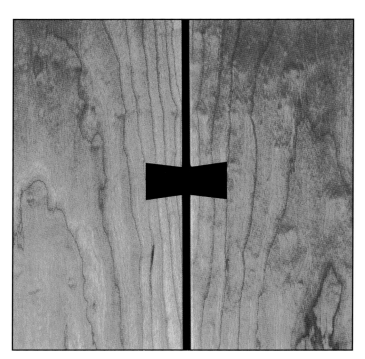

Photographer: Becky Stayner.

Kevin has three unique furniture lines, the Classic, Floating Top, and Glasgow series. In the early 1990s he collaborated with New York designer Cliff Young to develop the Classic series with its distinctively Post-Modern feel. The lines in this series are clean and simple with a Shaker influence.

Drawing inspiration from Frank Lloyd Wright and the Arts & Crafts movement, Kevin created the Floating Top series. This line harkens back to the aesthetics of the early Arts & Crafts Movement but with a twist. Kevin started out reproducing the strength and integrity of the designs of the era, but, as the work evolved, the design began to take on a Japanese flavor. Interestingly, with more research Kevin discovered a not so unlikely coincidence: Wright was an avid collector of Japanese prints named "ukiyo-e," which in Japanese means "pictures of the floating world." Kevin explains, "The floating world collection represents the multiculturalism that has become our

Floating Series bookcase. Wood: cherry, ebonized maple. Photographer: Becky Stayner.

<u>Kevin Kopil Furniture Design</u>

81

global identity as we enter the twenty-first century, our floating world."

The Glasgow Series reflects both the modern and the traditional and honors Charles Rennie Mackintosh, one of the Scottish godfathers of the Arts & Crafts Movement. Kevin came up with the series after an inspirational trip to the Museum of Modern Art for the Mackintosh retrospective.

Working exclusively with the finest Appalachian hardwoods, Kevin favors cherry and maple explaining that they are a "pleasure to work with and endowed with spectacular grains." Delicate contours, tapered arms and legs, and ebony inlay are some of the features that make Kevin's furniture distinctive.

Classic Series side chairs. Wood: cherry, tiger maple, ebonized maple. Chair seats: fabric. Photographer: Becky Stayner.

Classic Series nightstand.
Wood: cherry, ebony inlaid top.
Photographer: Becky Stayner.

Detail of nightstand.
Photographer: Becky Stayner.

Kevin Kopil Furniture Design

Right:
Detail of dining table.
Photographer: Becky Stayner.

Below:
Classic Series chairs and *Refectory* dining table.
Wood: cherry, maple. Chair seats: fabric.
Photographer: Becky Stayner.

<u>Kevin Kopil Furniture Design</u>

Gregg Lipton Furniture

"Create the highest, grandest vision possible for your
life because you become what you believe."
Oprah Winfrey

Creating something new and unique within the constraints of the design process is what inspires Gregg Lipton of Cumberland, Maine. Furniture that is used to relax, eat, read, work, sleep, and collect challenges Gregg not only to respond to functional needs, but also to create something of beauty. He finds the challenge of creating for a prescribed purpose invigorates him, whether it is for an upscale restaurant in New York, an inn in Kennebunkport, or Oprah Winfrey's Harpo Productions in Chicago.

Completely enamored with wood, he says it holds a "precious and sacred place in his psyche." He explains that wood engages all of his senses and commands his "respect, patience, and understanding." That is easily seen in each of his sophisticated designs.

Gregg's designs are influenced by three main aesthetics: the architect Frank Lloyd Wright, the Art Deco designs of Jacques Emile Ruhlmann, and, most recently, the simple and elegant designs of the Biedermeier Era. He doesn't wish to mimic the old designs, but instead uses their forms and redefines them in his own voice, always making sure, he says, that "simplicity of form" is the defining element of the piece. Each piece of furniture seems to have a musical quality about it that creates a union with the admirer.

Gregg Lipton (b. 1957). Photographer: Tonee Harbert.

Gregg embraces veneering as a design component that can lend additional depth to his forms. He says, "Not all of my work is veneer, but my most *interesting* work is. Veneering allows a designer the opportunity to leave the constraints of solid wood and traditional joinery. This allows me to push the limits with wood."

Born in St. Louis, Missouri, he moved to Maine 17 years ago after graduating from college with a degree in business. He thought he would return to school to study

Photographer: Dennis Griggs.

The mill where Gregg has his workshop, office, and showroom. Photographer: Tonee Harbert.

architecture, but realized he liked the smaller scale and detailing involved in creating furniture. This was a choice he emphatically says he does not regret. He loves to work with his hands and maintains that he is making tomorrow's antiques today.

His studio can be found in a restored 1860 water-powered lumber mill. It was a working mill until the 1940s, and later renovated into a home in the late 1950s. Now it not only serves as a workshop, office, and showroom for his furniture, but also a source of inspiration. Gregg has always had a dream of working and living on the same property, and a decade ago that dream was realized when he rode his bike down a winding, tree-lined road in Cumberland, and found his piece of the American dream.

Rocker Rocker. Wood: cherry.
Photographer: Stretch Tuemmler.

Keystone panel bed. Wood: curly maple. Photographer: Dennis Griggs.

Keystone sideboard. Wood: curly cherry. Metal: stainless steel.
Photographer: Stretch Tuemmler.

Gazelle II table. Wood: cherry. Metal: stainless steel.
Photographer: Dennis Griggs.

<u>Gregg Lipton Furniture</u>

Dining room setting. Wood: curly maple. Metal: stainless steel. Chair seats and backs: leather.
Photographer: Carey C. Marden.

Mack & Rodel Studio

"I try to make sense of things. Which is why, I guess, I believe in destiny. There must be a reason that I am as I am. There must be."
Andrew Martin, the robot from
the movie *Bicentennial Man*

Susan Mack and Kevin Rodel experienced show business firsthand, when they were asked to build eight chairs for Disney Studios' production of *Bicentennial Man*. They were paid in full prior to the project, rearranged their schedules to meet Disney's filming schedule, and FedExed the chairs overnight. They anxiously awaited the premier, only to discover the chairs that they had worked so diligently on appeared for only about 10 seconds, and then, to their disappointment, only the upper section of two chairs could be seen.

Movie "stardom" is not their only claim to fame, however. Kevin and Susan have been featured in several books, won awards, and lectured on the Arts & Crafts movement. Perhaps the most exciting recognition they have received was an invitation by the Glasglow School of Art to travel to Scotland to study the feasibility of producing facsimiles of several original Charles Rennie Mackintosh pieces. It was a grand experience for them. They thoroughly enjoyed studying the furniture firsthand, but in the end they realized it would be too much work without the assistance of additional employees. The experience also reinforced their love and passion for everything Arts & Crafts.

Kevin and Susan both grew up in Philadelphia and met because they shared a mutual interest in music and wood. Their decision to move to Maine and build furniture full-time was an easy one. They were both working as employees on a ship when they discovered not only the rugged beauty of Maine, but also the many furniture shops where they could apprentice. They both worked as assistants for well-known furniture maker Thos. Moser, before they took the leap to start their own business.

They do not consider their designs "original" but adaptations of Arts & Crafts designs that have evolved over time to better accommodate the requirements of today's lifestyles. They favor the philosophy and tenets of the movement and feel comfortable designing in that style, using only traditional joinery techniques.

A bygone finishing technique the couple uses for white oak is fuming. The method is rarely used today because of various environmental precautions. The completed item of furniture is exposed to vapors of concentrated ammonia in an airtight chamber. The vapors react with the tannins in the oak to naturally darken the wood. The longer the oak is exposed to the vapors, the darker the shade obtained. This procedure allows for different shade changes without compromising the rich grain of white oak with artificial pigmentations.

Kevin Rodel (b. 1949).
Photographer: Dennis Griggs.

Photographer: Dennis Griggs.

Kevin and Susan prefer to work by themselves. They have no plans to hire employees, unless their two sons would like to join them in their fulfilling livelihood. From initial wood selection to final finishing, each piece is meticulously crafted, allowing the beauty of the wood to be the essence of the piece.

With all the time and detail that goes into their furniture, it was no wonder they were disappointed to not have more of their chairs appear in the movie. When asked how he felt about it, Kevin merely replied, "Lesson learned – now I know why movie tickets cost so much!"

Glasgow sideboard. Wood: quartersawn white oak. Photographer: Dennis Griggs.

Facing Page:
Argyll server. Wood: quartersawn white oak. Additional
materials: tile, glass. Photographer: Dennis Griggs.

<u>Mack & Rodel Studio</u>

An Art & Crafts room setting. Bookcase, Morris chair, and tall book stand by Mack & Rodel Studio. Half-round table and painted clock by David Berman. Photographer: Dennis Griggs.

Argyll huntboard. Wood: quartersawn white oak. Tile: Lowe tiles. Photographer: Dennis Griggs.

Prairie desk. Wood: cherry. Panels: black leather. Photographer: Dennis Griggs.

Cerridwen bookcase. Wood: cherry, inlay. Photographer: Dennis Griggs.

<u>Mack & Rodel Studio</u>

Mission Evolution

"Life doesn't get any better than this."
Bill Bryson,
In a Sun Burned Country

Arnold d'Epagnier (b. 1955). Photographer: Michael Latil.

Photographer: Michael Latil.

Australia can be an interesting place to live, especially if you're a craftsman taking a year hiatus from the States. There are some definite challenges that need to be addressed, including learning to work with the local wood species, watching out for poisonous reptiles, and, of course, overcoming the language barrier. The quote "two countries separated by a common language" was never more apparent than when Arnold d'Epagnier began his stint as an Australian wood worker.

Arnold made the trek Down Under to build furniture for a childhood friend and her family, and found himself a bit perplexed after speaking with the locals. He says, "I met some 'woodies' (furniture makers), not to be confused with 'chippies' (carpenters). I was captivated by their beautiful woods, and thought I would make something quickly. I struggled with this heavy, dense board to get it to a friend's shed (shop) and asked if I could start. He said, 'Righto (yep), since it is not a big deal (wood plank) mate (bud). Pass it through the docka (cross cut saw), then run it through the buzza (joiner), put a surface on it (send it through the planer), then fit it out (cut joinery), and don't forget to vent (vacuum)." Arnold did not have a clue what was being said, and wondered if indeed they were talking about woodworking at all, he jokingly recalls.

However difficult it was to communicate at first, it didn't prevent Arnold from making a beautiful oval Australian red gum dining room set. The table featured a free-flowing design, which revealed an inlaid center with high back chairs to match. His friends were more than delighted with the final product.

Deciphering the Australian dialect has not been the only thing Arnold has figured out. A self-taught furniture maker, he is now enjoying national recognition. He was initially influenced by his father, an architect, who taught him respect and sympathy of design. Arnold explains why he chose this profession, "I enjoyed the design aspect and using my hands, mind, and heart that the furniture making process allows." When asked which wood he likes best, he replied, "The one I'm working with."

Inspired by Frank Lloyd Wright and the architectural designs of the Greene brothers, Arnold uses their vocabulary, but puts a decidedly modernist interpretation to it. Not content with imitating previous masters' work, Arnold infuses his furniture with subtle details and embellished joinery. He creates "practical, usable art furniture," complementing many pieces through detailed inlays, metalwork, marquetry, and rice paper shoji screens.

His precise care and detail is expressed in his dining room china cabinet. The piece is made of cherry in a Greene & Greene style. Corner joinery, seven inside draw

China cabinet. Wood: cherry, ebony, black-eyed susan inlay. Photographer: Michael Latil.

ers, and ebony plugs are used to define the cabinet. But perhaps most interesting are the floral inlays of black-eyed Susan, the state flower of his home state Maryland, delicately placed on each side.

Whether he is braving the Outback or adding subtle details to a maple table, perhaps what kindles Arnold's passion the most is furniture that emulates "some early childhood dream experience, sitting in large wooden Arts & Crafts furniture by a boulder fireplace, cooling in the shadows with iced tea listening to adults and a nearby brook babble on."

Right:
Detail of Art Nouveau butterfly table.
Photographer: Michael Latil.

Below:
Art Nouveau butterfly table. Wood: quilted maple, walnut.
Paper: rice paper. Photographer: Michael Latil.

Captain's bed. Wood: cherry. Photographer: Michael Latil.

Australian Dining table and chairs. Wood: Australian sheoak, huon pine, ebony. Photographer: Michael Latil.

China cabinet. Wood: quartersawn white oak. Metal: inlay. Photographer: Michael Latil.

Nojo Design

"Sometimes your life comes into focus one frame at a time."
from the movie *The Majestic*

Jo R. Roessler (b. 1970). Photographer: Jo Roessler.

"My strongest conviction is staying true to my design and vision," says furniture maker and Landmark Majestic Theatre owner, Jo Roessler. Jo and his wife, Nora, bought the historic theatre in Easthampton, Massachusetts in early 2001. The structure was built in 1923 and had been left vacant since the early 1990s. They have renovated the space that now houses the new workshop for Nojo Design. The Majestic is approximately 9,000 square feet divided into workshops and two store fronts. The front gallery will showcase an area for art and fine furniture. The building's new design was a collaborative effort between father and son. Jo's father, an architect specializing in historical preservation, designed the renovation.

His father has always fueled his interest in construction. "As long as I can remember," Jo recalls, "I have been intensely fascinated with the construction of everyday objects." As his tastes matured, the fascination grew to love of design, "which naturally progressed into an interest in furniture making." He also adds that part of that fascination was the interaction between user and object.[1]

His first furniture making experience evolved out of necessity, and his initial pieces were made of metal, not wood. Jo went to college to study photography. He needed a way to exhibit his photos, so he began to construct elaborate boxes to display them in. He switched from metal to wood for its organic qualities, favoring the warmth and grain characteristics of wood to the cold sterile metal. Enamored with the idea of creating something three-dimensional that people could handle, as opposed to something that just hangs on a wall, Jo shifted his focus to furniture making.

His designs are a reflection of an Asian style, with subtle, unexpected elements. Many pieces surprise you. Sometimes

Photographer: Jo Roessler.

Entertainment center. Wood: walnut, crotch walnut panels. Photographer: Jo Roessler.

Dining room table and chairs. Wood: cherry, walnut accents. Chair seats: leather.
Photographer: Jo Roessler.

Sideboard. Wood: cherry, walnut. Photographer: Jo Roessler.

he will put a drawer on top of a case piece instead of below or divide a drawer space into thirds instead of halves. He works mostly in cherry with walnut or maple accents. For Jo, the process of design is looking for the essence of the wood. Like a sculptor, he looks for what needs to be taken away and what needs to remain so the piece might emerge from the wood. Every day, Jo strives to find timeless forms and aesthetic accessibility in his work. His enjoyment is in the idea that his furniture can be a work of art that people will interact with on a daily basis.

Bar stools. Wood: maple, cherry. Photographer: Jo Roessler.

Cabinet. Wood: cherry, red oak. Photographer: Jo Roessler.

Cabinet. Wood: cherry, maple, curly maple. Photographer: Jo Roessler.

Charles Shackleton
Furniture

"Fortitudine Vincimus — By endurance we conquer."
Ernest Shackleton,
family motto

Setting a goal of excellence and nothing less is not an original concept for the Shackletons. Coming from a long line of overachievers, Charles Shackleton has put his own mark on history. A direct descendant of David Ricardo, the famous economist of the mid-18th century, and the Anglo-Irish Antarctic explorer, Sir Ernest Shackleton, Charles has success in his blood.

Born near Dublin, Ireland, Charles went to art school at West Surrey College of Art & Design in Farnum, England, where he studied in a variety of media. Desiring to find a career that would satisfy his physical and spiritual needs, he chose the path that he had gravitated toward as a child. He discovered that his childhood passion of creating things with his hands seemed to feed his soul like nothing else. He found "enlightenment, freedom, healing, happiness, timelessness, imagination, inspiration, fulfillment, and peace," he says, during the many hours he spent in an old workshop behind his parents' house. Charles explains the process, "What exactly it is that leads one into this world, I do not know. It is something to do with creating. Using hand tools to

Charles Shackleton (b. 1958). Photographer: Thomas Ames Jr.

Photographer: Thomas Ames Jr.

Interior of workshop. Photographer: Thomas Ames Jr.

Carved kitchen dresser. Wood: cherry. Photographer: Thomas Ames Jr.

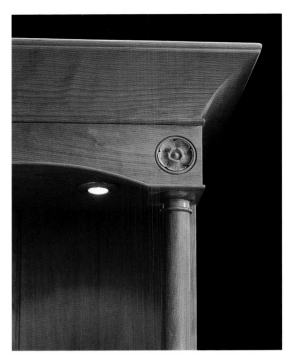

Crown molding detail.
Photographer: Thomas Ames Jr.

create many shapes, sticking these shapes together to create new shapes, and bringing it all together creating something that goes far beyond the sum of all those parts." Whatever it is, Charles has been able to turn a childhood escape into the lucrative company of his dreams.

He began his career not as a furniture maker, but as a glassblower. After art school he went to work in Ireland for the famed glassblower, Simon Pearce, who introduced Charles to the intricacies of the glassblowing process. When Simon left Ireland to start a glassblowing studio and shop in Quechee, Vermont, Charles quickly followed.

The time spent with Simon gave him insight into *fluidity,* a term not often used in furniture making. It's an idea that helped Charles to express the thoughts and ideas he often felt while crafting. For Charles it is about leading others to a place he found to be educational, yet whimsical, like traveling to another time or another world in your own mind, and then interpreting it through a bed, a chair, or a table. His furniture seems to carry a regal quality not unlike the furniture of the Louis XVI era. He describes his sleigh bed, with its elegant and

The Shackleton showroom. Photographer: Thomas Ames Jr.

<u>Charles Shackleton Furniture</u>

Extending pedestal dining table and chairs. Wood: cherry. Chair seats: fabric. Photographer: Thomas Ames Jr.

upright curls and magnificent curves, as something Napoleon would have laid back on.

Oddly enough, working with his friend Josh Metcalf was his only professional woodworking experience. Through Charles's tenure with Josh he learned the use of hand tools and, as he puts it, "to use my brain!" Formal training or not, he seems to have an innate ability to know what is important in design and function. For instance, with his rocker he explains that he wanted, "something with a lot of character and a lot of handwork, but quite simple...to be very comfortable and rock nicely." For the most part, his designs are interpretations of classic styles, approaching every task with the thorough process of comfort, aesthetic, and functionality.

It is important to mention that Charles feels strongly about not making the piece too finished so that it looks like it came out of a factory. Charles's assistants use hand planes extensively to accentuate the feel of each piece. He asks the question, "Why make a piece perfectly smooth as if a machine did all the work?" Why indeed. The tactile quality of Charles's work has won the hearts of many clients who wish to make a connection with the craftsman who lovingly and carefully hand-planed each piece.

Arm chair detail.
Photographer: Thomas Ames Jr.

Charles Shackleton Furniture

Raymond Bock
Woodworking

"It must be manifest that an ornamental design will be more beautiful if it seems part of the surface or substance that receives it than if it looks 'stuck on,' so to speak."

Louis Sullivan,
Kindergarten Chats

Ornament to me is as physically functional as legs on a table." That's why Raymond Bock uses three to four different woods on each of his pieces. He chooses to use contrasting wood to draw the onlooker's eye to certain areas and highlights. Raymond intertwines his furniture with a sense of whimsy, with curvaceous backs and rounded legs.

Like many wood artisans, Raymond didn't start out as a woodworker. His first love was photography, a hobby he continues today by photographing all of his own work. He majored in photography at the Illinois Institute of Technology in Chicago, a school that has its roots in the Bauhaus school of thought.

The most notable faculty member at IIT was Ludwig Mies van der Rohe. An architect by trade, van der Rohe was the Director of the Bauhaus School in Germany from 1930 to 1933 before the Nazis shut the school down. The Bauhaus represented the ideals of a brave new world and the stripping away of ornament, historical references, and regional differences. Instead, it stressed the importance of "pure design," without reference to the human touch. Production was the main focus rather than natural materials and human craftsmanship. The style was summed

Raymond Bock (b. 1953). Photographer: Ray Bock.

Photographer: Ray Bock.

Exterior of workshop.
Photographer: Ray Bock.

Swivel stool. Wood: cherry, curly maple. Chair seat: leather. Photographer: Ray Bock.

<u>Raymond Bock Woodworking</u>

up in van der Rohe's proclamation "less is more." He traveled to Chicago to serve as Director of Architecture at IIT in 1938.

Fortunately Raymond holds a different view. Each of his pieces is handcrafted using the beauty of the wood, often choosing cherry, curly maple, walnut, or oak. He designs each piece and then constructs it himself, to be sure the furniture is made just the way he wants it. Much time and care goes into the making of every piece of furniture.

He shuns exotic woods in favor of North American hardwoods. He explains that it is as much a "self-imposed design parameter as it is an environmental concern," maintaining that he prefers the piece to focus around the design rather than the exotic or the glitzy. Just as important to his work is his design philosophy. He describes it as a fun tug-of-war between his educational background and his natural urges. His schooling stressed very clean, minimal design in which "aesthetics flow out of function," while Raymond leans toward integrating some nonfunctional elements.

Finding Chicago too frenetic, he moved to the pastoral setting of Wisconsin just after college. He now lives in Viroqua with his wife and two children, who provide him with daily inspiration.

Right:
Hall table detail. Photographer: Ray Bock.

Below:
Hall table. Wood: American sycamore, English sycamore, cherry. Photographer: Ray Bock.

<u>Raymond Bock Woodworking</u>

Sideboard. Wood: quartersawn white oak, cherry, maple. Photographer: Ray Bock.

Desk. Wood: cherry, curly maple, walnut. Photographer: Ray Bock.

<u>Raymond Bock Woodworking</u>

Doerr Woodworking

"Sailing is just the bottom line, like adding up the score in bridge. My real interest is in the tremendous game of life."
Dennis Conner, yachtsman

Michael Doerr of Sturgeon Bay, Wisconsin, considers himself a functional artist, one who has received great guidance and inspiration from those who have walked the path of craft before him. He began his solo business in 1989, crafting his original design of tables and chairs.

Michael's first introduction to woodworking was many years ago when he was in his mid-twenties. He began as a wooden shipwright for the famed boat builder, Fred Nimphius, a man Michael considers to be one of the most influential figures in shaping him into the furniture maker he is today. Fred was not only Michael's boss but also his mentor, who often said, "It is not what you accomplish in a day but what you learn from a day's work." Michael describes the master/apprentice relationship as a dance where knowledge is passed on from generation to generation.

Some other seminal figures in Michael's interesting life are modern master Sam Maloof and architect Frank Lloyd Wright. Their contributions are easily seen in Michael's No. 1 chair. Viewing it in profile, one can easily detect the stacked planes running out into space, which is Wright's influence, while the sculptural lines of Maloof's influence cause the eye to flow throughout the piece.

Michael Doerr (b. 1952). Photographer: Jeff Davis.

Photographer: Matt Othober.

Another life lesson Michael learned from both Maloof and Nimphius, he says, is to work to the best of his ability and with integrity. With the love and good advice of his wife Bobbi, Michael tries to do just that with every piece he makes. His passion and desire is to create objects of beauty. He describes his style of work as an "outgrowth of my lifestyle and previous influences." He goes on to say that, "Gathering information and accepting or rejecting it is a great part of life." He maintains that even in rejection you can find influence.

Michael is a one-man operation. Never starting with a drawing, he goes straight to the wood for his muse. The process begins

Hanging cradle. Wood: cherry. Photographer: Frank Riemer.

Dining table and chairs. Wood: walnut.
Photographer: Frank Riemer.

with hand selecting each board. Then the boards are fitted together like a puzzle to create an outline of a cube. Next, he says, he "takes away everything that doesn't look like a chair." With every object he makes he is sure to create a flowing, unbroken line that draws the eye around the chair or table. These details can be time-consuming. Each chair takes between 20-25 hours to build, before several more hours of sanding and buffing. When finished, every chair is signed and numbered.

The No. 1 Chair. Wood: yellow birch. Photographer: Matt Othober.

Bobbi's chair. Wood: curly maple.
Photographer: Matt Othober.

Pedestal table with *Bobbi's* chairs. Wood: curly maple.
Photographer: Matt Othober.

G. Keener & Co.

"That a man may show the love of God in his work he must be free."

Eric Gill,
A Holy Tradition of Working

Gary Keener is living the American dream. He shares a farmhouse with his wife Andrea and their newborn daughter in a small, rural Ohio town. There are not many other houses around. It is quiet and peaceful except for the occasional bark from his black Labs. Actually the only thing missing in this Countrytime Lemonade setting is a hammock hanging from the big mulberry tree. He works in a shop next to his house, located just a few feet from his front door.

This picturesque lifestyle was not something that came easily or something he always knew he wanted. It was through trial and error (like many of us) that Gary stumbled upon his honest livelihood. Gary remarks that he, like many woodworkers, has always been drawn to creating and building things out of wood. At an early age

Gary Keener (b. 1974). Photographer: Jill Markwood.

Photographer: Jill Markwood.

he could often be found nailing pieces of wood together. He was usually dreaming up new ideas that he would later turn into toy trucks or, in one case, an entire farm made out of scrap wood. Using raw materials and then turning them into something both beautiful and functional was what initially motivated him and would help dictate the career he would later pursue.

Gary's love for designing and creating caused him to take an industrial arts class in high school. He was fortunate to have an exceptional teacher who taught his students the skills to transform wood and motivated them to excellence. An accomplished woodworker himself, Gary's teacher knew how to pass knowledge on to other generations and continually preached that nothing was unachievable.

After high school Gary went to college, not for woodworking, but for teaching. He wanted to emulate his high school industrial arts teacher who had influenced him so much. He desired to teach young people and pass on

Facing page:
Chimney cupboard. Wood: cherry, curly maple, walnut. Photographer: Jill Markwood.

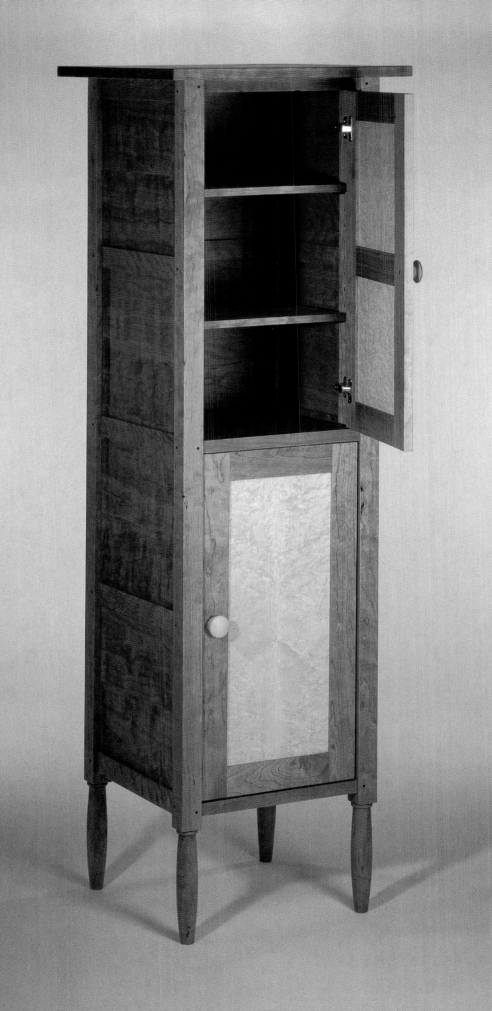

Dining table and chairs. Wood: cherry, maple. Chair seats: fabric. Photographer: Amy Stapleton.

the knowledge that he had gained. As a teacher, Gary enjoyed developing pride in his students and nurturing their creativity. He assumed that he would spend the next thirty years of his life teaching, then retire and continue to build furniture as a hobby.

Not long into his career, he received several commissions to build furniture and found that he enjoyed building furniture more than he did teaching. Andrea encouraged him to leave the teaching profession to craft furniture full time. With her support and encouragement he applied for a furniture apprenticeship with well-known furniture maker M.T. Maxwell in Virginia.

While there, he was able to develop his own style and techniques.

Gary's furniture is reflective of the Shaker style. Simple, uncomplicated lines with straightforward durability, combined with traditional Shaker design principles and joinery techniques. His pieces have been featured in trade magazines for their unique look and functionality.

Gary may have decided to take an unconventional approach to his work, but he hasn't given up his spiritual values. His faith in Christ is strong and his values are reflected in all that he does. From his family, to his design principles, Gary seems to be on the right path.

Armoire. Wood: cherry, walnut.
Photographer: Jill Markwood.

Armoire (open). Photographer: Jill Markwood.

G. Keener & Co.

Sideboard. Wood: cherry, walnut accents. Photographer: Amy Stapleton.

Bed. Wood: cherry. Photographer: Jill Markwood.

G. Keener & Co.

Charles Radtke
Furniture Maker

"My imagination is a monastery and I am its monk."
John Keats

Charles Radtke believes his work needs to speak for itself. He has never been a fan of drawing people into his furniture by telling a story, but prefers the wood and form communicate. Charles explains, "It is not relevant to the work that the lumber was (for instance) submerged in Lake Superior." He feels the real concerns to be, "How was it worked? And did it turn into something stunning?" Charles maintains that the real story is in the grain patterns, colors, and the way light is reflected.

Charles's story begins in Hermann, Missouri, with ten siblings. He describes his fondest childhood memories as being defined by music and literature. His father, a butcher, taught him the importance of not being afraid to fail. His father was never satisfied, and continually modified his techniques to keep striving for perfection. Charles is reminded of this daily as he works toward perfection

Charles Radtke (b. 1964). Photographer: Doug Edmunds.

in his own pieces. Charles says that you can be a bit too brazen if you don't know what you're doing. "One pass of the hand plane too many and it's gone forever,"[1] he says regarding color and grain patterns. There are so many intricacies. "All that lies within the wood,"[2] Charles explains, and "removing a plane shaving you can read a newspaper through will change a grain pattern."[3]

He got his first glimpse into furniture making while working nights at a Catholic friary in Oakbrook, Illinois, where his brother, a Franciscan monk, was stationed. It was there that he made his first piece of furniture. The furniture was "bulky and fairly Gothic looking"[4] but it captured his heart. Later Charles studied under James Krenov to learn the techniques of a modern master while acquiring his own unique style and technique.

Admiring his furniture is a true pleasure, specifically his *Inner Light Series*. In these exquisitely crafted cabinets Charles has created a way to allow light into the closed cabinet by setting the top slightly apart from the base. This causes light to shine out from the front doors and illuminate the cabinet at the same time.

Photographer: Doug Edmunds.

Music Cabinet Number One. Wood: cherry, bloodwood. Metal: enameled copper by Sarah Perkins.
Photographer: Doug Edmunds.

Charles Radtke Furniture Maker

Sarcophagus Number One. Wood: sassafras, mahogany. Metal: brass.
Photographer: Doug Edmunds.

Incidentally, his favorite furniture to design and build are his freestanding cabinets. Charles says, "When I look at a piece of wood, I am immediately asking myself…what kind of cabinet might come from this?"[5] In fact he finds it the most intriguing furniture in the home. "They hold things…secrets. I'm drawn to that,"[6] Charles says, adding that a cabinet is interactive; you have to touch it, open it, manipulate it, work with it.[7] He is very particular about not just the "aesthetics, the proportions, but all the moving parts as well."[8]

Being sensitive to all possibilities is something h[e] picked up at the friary. Because the monks build every[thing] they need, from doors, to rooms, to the furniture he is able to check the functionality – even if that mean[s] from the inside of a cabinet. "A piece can be beautifu[l] with nontraditional wood and graceful lines, but if it i[s] not functional, it just won't work." First and foremost h[e] makes a cabinet to be used. "It should please you whe[n] you handle it. If it happens to be beautiful when you'r[e] not using it, so much the better,"[9] he says.

Inner Light Number Three cabinet. Wood: tiger walnut, hard maple.
Photographer: Doug Edmunds.

Velde chair. Wood: cherry, maple. Chair fabric: Unika Vaev.
Photographer: Doug Edmunds.

Inner Light Number Two cabinet. Wood: walnut, persimmon. ~~aper~~ Paper: handmade paper. Photographer: Jack Weissman.

Inner Light Number Two cabinet — open. Photographer: Jack Weissman.

Lorna Secrest

"Neither birth nor sex forms a limit to genius."
Charlotte Bronte

"Where's the person who really made this?" "What does your husband need this tool for?" These are two of the many remarks regarding her furniture that Lorna Secrest has had to endure over the years. Unfortunately, too many people are surprised to discover that the elegant and magnificently crafted furniture before them has been built by a woman. Upon meeting her, one can be a bit taken aback; she is a small, friendly woman with bright eyes and a shy demeanor. But making things is in her blood. Her father makes jewelry and stained glass, and both her parents owned a lucrative craft gallery in Petoskey, Michigan, while she was growing up.

Lorna turns lumber into playful yet exquisite beds, chairs, and tables. Her grasp of texture and color is evident in her ability to contrast light woods with wrought iron, ebony, or glass, resulting in a fresh approach and bold ideas.

Barely in her forties, Lorna has created volumes of case pieces, beds, tables, chairs, and bookshelves all uniquely designed to meet each customer's personal specification. Describing her work would require a description of each and every one of her clients, for all of

Lorna Secrest (b. 1959). Photographer: Author.

Photographer:
Lorna Secrest.

Club chair and ottoman. Wood: pear. Upholstery: fabric.
Photographer: Lorna Secrest.

Bed. Wood: purpleheart. Additional material: composition leaf.
Photographer: Lorna Secrest.

her work is custom and tailored to the individual's needs. Lorna effortlessly balances the playful and functional.

Most of her pieces are made of both solid wood and veneers. Lorna's specialty is in creating complex and intricate veneers and inlays, often choosing several wood species to complement one another. Lorna says she "enjoys using veneers because of the range of texture and color they provide." She maintains that "veneers are a better use of wood environmentally," explaining one can yield far more out of one log when using thin sheets of veneer.

When asked how she would describe her furniture, she says, "My pieces are created through exploration of a wide variety of decorative art movements. By combining design elements with marketability, I try to create pieces with integrity that will function within parameters set by craftsperson and client." Lorna draws inspiration from many historical styles and designers. Some of her favorites are Charles Rennie Mackintosh, the father of the Arts & Crafts Movement in Scotland, the abstract and geometric designs of Joseph Hoffman, and Art Deco artisan Edgar Brandt.

Like her distinctive furniture, Lorna, too, is unconventional. She began her furniture business at the young age of 23 in 1983. This would be quite a challenge for anyone, let alone a woman in an industry dominated by men. Her interests stem from elective courses in woodworking she took during her first few semesters at Rochester Institute of Technology in Rochester, New York. Though she started out as a textile major, she switched during her sophomore year. She thrived on the constant challenge of transforming a drawing on paper into a three-dimensional object. She also discovered that she enjoyed working with the different textures of wood species. Gutsy and artistic, Lorna can dream up a piece of furniture that surprises, intrigues, and makes you smile, all at the same time.

Bedroom interior. Photographer: Lorna Secrest.

Dining table and chairs. Wood: bubinga, birdseye maple, pear. Seats: fabric. Photographer: Lorna Secrest.

<u>Lorna Secrest</u>

Side table. Wood: curly maple, pear, holly. Photographer: Lorna Secrest.

Living room interior. Photographer: Lorna Secrest.

<u>Lorna Secrest</u>

Brian Boggs Chairmakers

"Tho' the moment be cloudy or fair. Let us trust in our Savior away.
Who keepeth everyone in His care."
From the sound track of
O Brother, Where Art Thou?

In a sleepy area of Kentucky known as Berea, Brian Boggs has quietly become known as one of the country's foremost chair makers. He traveled to the area to learn woodworking at Berea College. Upon arrival, Brian was surprised and disappointed to learn that most of the woodworking focus was on power tools and not hand tool training. He eventually switched majors to French and philosophy, before dropping out of college to teach himself furniture making.

Brian was deeply impacted by the book *Make a Chair from a Tree*, by John D. Alexander. He was fascinated by the idea of the ability to fell a tree and have the final product be a beautiful, well-crafted chair. With only hand tools, Brian decided to concentrate on the chair because "it was the cheapest way to set up a shop, and there aren't any requirements for real straight lines or flat surfaces."[1] With little money, no power tools, and no formal training (and a baby on the way), Brian began exploring the way Appalachian chairs were traditionally made. Most Appalachian chair makers were not professional chair makers, rather they used their abilities for supplemental income during the winter months.

Over the years the Appalachian chair has changed little in form and technique. The chairs are put together with wet-dry joinery, which begins with slightly damp legs and very dry rungs. The damp mortise and dry tenon form an extremely tight joint when the differing moisture contents reach equilibrium. Brian made a hundred Appalachian post-and-rung chairs, and then headed for Vermont to learn how to make Windsor chairs. The difference is in the construction. The post-and-rung chair legs are continuous, and the Windsor chair has a thick wood seat that the legs, spindles, and back supports socket into.

After making over 20 Windsor chairs, Brian found that he had come to a crossroads in his career. He knew the Appalachian post-and-rung chair was where his heart was, but he didn't want to give up on what he had learned about the Windsor chair.

Brian Boggs (b. 1959). Photographer: Geoff Carr.

Photographer: Dave Zurick.

Brian decided to merge the two chair designs. He began making an arrow-back chair in his own unique style by combining the Appalachian post-and-rung and Windsor styles. Brian now makes a variety of chair styles. His most popular are the ladder back, fan back, and a woven hickory bark back. He uses only Appalachian hardwoods such as walnut, cherry, oak, hickory, and maple.

One of Brian's biggest challenges is to find good raw materials for his chairs, especially quality hickory bark for his seats.

He has designed a machine that will take the raw hickory bark and, after many passes through the machine, produce the final material needed for the woven seats and backs. Brian must coordinate his work with local loggers to obtain lumber when they cut it down; otherwise he would have to fell the tree himself. All of the work must be done in the middle of the woods, which becomes an extremely labor intensive process.

Brian has demonstrated his skills at the Smithsonian Institute's Museum for Craft, the Renwick Gallery. He has also been featured in many woodworking magazines and has appeared on the PBS program *The American Wood Shop*. He developed a spokeshave (a tool to shape curved work) and frequently lectures across the United States on how to make his chairs.

Perhaps the greatest testament to Brian's chair making acumen and ability was in 1988 when Sam Maloof, the great American craftsman, purchased a chair. Sam liked the chair so much he eventually bought two more and a footstool.

Left:
Woven-back chair. Wood: ebonized white oak, hickory bark. Photographer: Geoff Carr.

Below:
Woven-back chair detail. Photographer: Geoff Carr.

Facing Page:
Fan-back chair. Wood: ebonized maple, maple. Chair seat: leather. Photographer: Geoff Carr.

Dining table and chairs. Wood: walnut. Chair seat: hickory bark. Photographer: Geoff Carr.

Settee. Wood: ebonized white oak.
Chair seat: hickory bark.
Photographer: Geoff Carr.

Woven-back rocker. Wood: cherry.
Chair seat and back: hickory bark.
Photographer: Geoff Carr.

<u>Brian Boggs Chairmakers</u>

Michael Colca
Furniture Maker

"If you enjoy what you do, you'll never work a day in your life."

Confucius

Michael Colca is a unique orator with the gift of eloquence, capable of articulating what many can only execute. He is able to put into words the passions and intricacies of the furniture making process so profoundly that any who are listening can obtain a clear understanding of why he does what he does. Talking with him, one is able to gain valuable insight into the heart of a craftsman.

As it turns out, his fascination began not with the wood itself, but with a person. Michael's early interest in building was piqued as a child, when he would often watch his neighbor, an engineer, come home and spend countless hours crafting beautiful pieces of furniture for his family. It was the dedication and joy his neighbor exhibited while tinkering away that caused Michael to be captivated with creating beautiful objects of his own.

Michael Colca (b. 1952). Photographer: Reagan Upshaw.

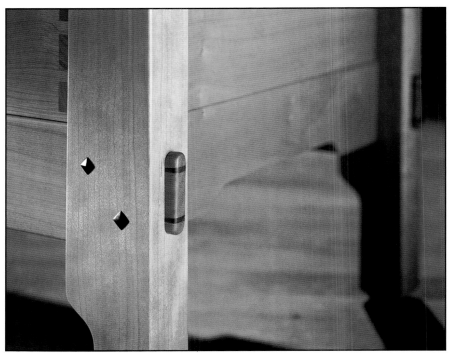

Photographer: Andrew Yates.

By 1977, Michael had already begun his life pursuit. His first job as a cabinetmaker in Austin, Texas, supplied him with the groundwork for a productive career, although the work wasn't quite what interested him. In addition to making cabinets, the shop also made skateboards and lots of them. "I knew it wasn't a place I was going to stay for long." He soon left the cabinet shop in pursuit of higher learning to build upon his skills and expand his knowledge.

Just a year later, he started his own cabinet shop in Driftwood, Texas, making fine cabinets while slowly but increasingly gaining commissions for unique furniture pieces. Michael explains that his designs are original in the

Treisman Highboy. Wood: mahogany. Photographer: Dewey Mears.

Medina trestle table, dining chairs and buffet. Wood: cherry. Chair seats: fabric. Photographer: Andrew Yates.

sense that he draws them and then builds them, but not without the inspiration from those who have gone before. He says he is "indebted to all those past and present who have explored this craft and put forth their best for the rest of us to study and critique." With heavy influence from the designs of California architects Charles and Henry Greene, his pieces exhibit a profound statement that inspires the observer.

His infusion of the Greene & Greene design is evident in his Medina collection. Believing that we are partners with nature, he tries to keep his designs "simple and free of any noise" that would distract from the wood itself. His Treisman Highboy is a perfect example, and is one of his most cherished designs. It was made for a client who wanted a place to display his Chinese tea pots.

Each of the elements — the drawer-pulls, the inlaid diamonds, the muntins and mullions, and the dovetails in the drawers are all carefully sized. "The result of the meticulous process," Michael says, "is harmony without repetition."

Michael and his only assistant, Mark Love, craft furniture in a quiet area of Texas. Michael wishes to respect the continuum of craft. "The finest work of human hands gives us a glimpse of eternal beauty. To build a thing by hand is a privilege. Through the work of those who have come before comes inspiration and a quest for perfection. Through my work, I hope to pass what I have received to those who follow me. My goal is to create work that will inspire, work that can be used and enjoyed now and for years to come."

<u>Michael Colca Furniture Makers</u>

140

Detail of arm chair.
Photographer: Andrew Yates.

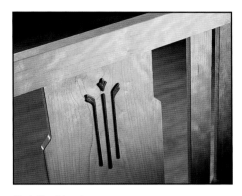

Detail of bed.
Photographer: Andrew Yates.

Medina bedroom. Wood: cherry, ebony. Photographer: Andrew Yates.

Michael Colca Furniture Makers

Medina writing desk. Wood: Texas pecan. Photographer: Reagan Upshaw.

Probst Furniture Makers

"Tree at my window, window tree,
My sash is lowered when night comes on;
But let there never be curtain drawn
Between you and me."

Robert Frost

Deep in the holler of the West Virginia coal mining country, a craftsman creates his own blend of Mission and Japanese influenced furniture. Surprisingly, his furniture exhibits an amazing array of graceful lines and elegant proportions. That is not something one would expect to see in one of the poorest counties of West Virginia. Jim Probst, originally from Indianapolis, moved to the Appalachians in the late 1970s in response to the "back to the land" movement.

As a junior at Ball State he happened to read *Living the Good Life* by Scott and Helen Nearing. It was a personal account of living off the land. The book encouraged the idea of retreating from suburbia and moving to rural areas to use the natural resources. Discovery of the book came at an opportune time because Jim had arrived at a crossroads in his young life. He was studying to be a teacher, but at the time there was a glut of teachers and many of Jim's friends who earned teaching degrees were taking jobs in factories.

Dropping out of college, he and his wife, Glenda (an accomplished weaver), journeyed to West Virginia in a search

Jim Probst (b. 1950). Photographer: Brad Feinknopf.

for land on which to settle. They found 112 acres many miles from any metropolis and about 45 minutes from Huntington or Charleston, West Virginia. They returned to work in Indiana for the next two years to pay for the newly acquired land. During this time Jim began to work as a carpenter. This was a choice inspired from his father who was an accomplished wood carver.

When they made the move to West Virginia in 1983, Jim began his career as a furniture maker with no electricity, water, or indoor plumbing. Determined to live off the land, Jim recounts a time when he rerouted a spring so that the fresh water would feed into the house. Bathing was managed by heating buckets of water on a wood burning stove.

Jim began making cabinets full time in a shed located on his property. It was from these modest beginnings that Jim found his true calling. As orders increased he gradually added porch swings, blanket chests, and small boxes to his repertoire.

Photographer: Brad Feinknopf.

Dora bedroom set. Wood: cherry, birdseye maple panels and drawer fronts. Photographer: Brad Feinknopf.

In his current 9,000 square foot location, Jim is just five miles from his homestead. He has shifted his focus entirely to furniture. Inside this concrete block building Jim and his only assistant, Vester Walsh, create carefully designed and constructed furniture. "Mission is popular at the moment," explains Jim, "but I think I came up with an individual style, and it's being well received." His furniture lines include the Otto and Dora Collections, named after his grandfather and grandmother. Contemporary, yet adhering to the construction techniques of 100 years ago, his unique Otto series fits just as easily in a Manhattan loft as it would in a California bungalow. The Dora series is appropriately more feminine, imparting sinuous lines with birdseye maple accents.

Upon close inspection Jim's reputation for attention to detail cannot be disputed. The joinery is seamless, finishes are like satin, and construction is sound. But it is perhaps his design acumen that has garnered the most recognition. "Different people ask me where I went to school and studied woodworking," Jim says. "They are very surprised when I tell them I taught myself."

Although now a nationally respected craftsman, Jim still remains true to his original beliefs. He and his family continue to live on the land he purchased almost thirty years ago. It is an area that has an abundance of oak, maple, walnut, and cherry. He has added plumbing and electricity but still has concern for giving back to the environment. "I'm a big proponent of developing the local wood industry," Jim explains. "I think we should try to promote wood more than coal because wood is a renewable resource. We can build an industry which will be here for our children and grandchildren – if we're careful and plant timber."

Otto dining set. Wood: cherry, ebonized cherry. Chair seats: black leather. Photographer: Brad Feinknopf.

Probst Furniture Makers

Otto hutch. Wood: cherry, ebonized cherry. Photographer: Brad Feinknopf.

Below:
Dora dining set. Wood: cherry, birdseye maple.
Photographer: Brad Feinknopf.

Right:
Detail of *Dora* dining set. Photographer: Brad
Feinknopf.

Dora sideboard. Wood: cherry, birdseye maple panels and drawer fronts.
Photographer: Brad Feinknopf.

White Wind Woodworking

"See, I was born and raised in Texas, and it means so
much to me. (That's right, you're not from Texas.)"
Lyle Lovett

For many who work in the depersonalized corporate world, woodworking can be a romantic ven-
ture. But for Daniel Kagay of Austin, Texas, the romanti-
cism lies in the personal relationships he develops
throughout the process rather than in the building itself.
He hasn't lost his passion for woodworking, but over the
past 30 years he has found that working with the client
has become equally important. "Translating a customer's
need into a three-dimensional object requires more that
just the ability or craftsmanship of working wood," he
explains. "In a sense it is a collaborative educational effort between maker and client." He describes how it is
not only important to have a common vocabulary, but
that mutual respect and trust are paramount. The clients
need to put their trust in the maker's ability to carry out
the plan, and the craftsperson needs to respect the clients' risk and faith in them.

Daniel also had to have a lot of faith in himself. After
graduating from the University of Texas at Austin with a

Daniel Kagay (b. 1953). Photographer: Ron Whitfield.

BA in History, he left for the east coast. Daniel had met
Richard Brown and his wife, Laura, at the university, and
it was through their friendship that he made frequent trips
to Boston to work on redoing a brownstone for the couple.

In Boston the "studio" furniture movement was rag-
ing. Daniel began to take note of the works of such masters as James Krenov, Wendell Castle, and Jere Osgood.
He had an affinity for building projects ever since he
worked on house construction during summer jobs in

Photographer: Ron Whitfield.

GW dining table and chairs. Wood: maple, ebony. Stone: granite. Table top: glass. Photographer: Ron Whitfield.

Detail of *GW* dining table. Photographer: Ron Whitfield.

<u>White Wind Woodworking</u>

high school. His first project was building a counter balance loom from a purchased plan. Its success encouraged further exploration.

As Daniel continued to travel back and forth to help the Browns on various projects, he was offered a position at the Massachusetts College of Art. Daniel says he enjoyed teaching, but "I like what I do now. Being in an ivory tower is a much different experience than trying to pay the bills each month." It was a time that Daniel remembers fondly. "It was an excuse to get out of my shop and become reenergized."

Now, Daniel has returned to Austin and has recently begun to explore new avenues. He says, "I have been working in wood for 30 years, and I am starting to explore more veneering. I began as a woodworker in the 60s. I am part of the hippie tradition with the focus on joinery and solid wood construction, but I now look at veneering as expanding possibilities."

Like his Texas roots, his furniture uses bold textures and wood species to cause a dramatic juxtaposition. Whether it is granite, glass and ebony, or recovered cypress and copper, Daniel blends contemporary elements with old-world craftsmanship.

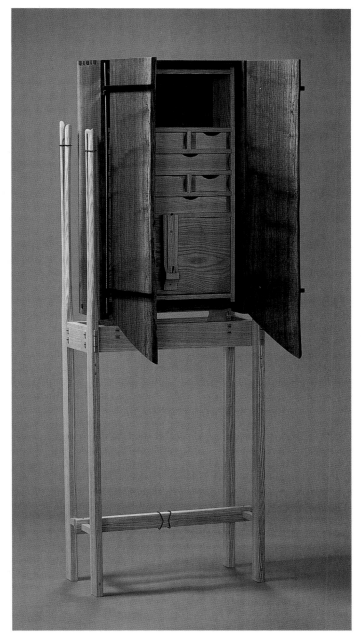

Collector's case. Wood: recovered heart pine, walnut. Photographer: Ron Whitfield.

Collector's case — open. Photographer: Ron Whitfield.

<u>White Wind Woodworking</u>

Left:
Detail of kitchen cabinets. Photographer: Ron Whitfield.

Below:
Culinary Altar & kitchen cabinets. Wood: maple.
Photographer: Ron Whitfield.

<u>White Wind Woodworking</u>

Berkeley Mills

"Clouds now and again
give a soul some respite from
moon-gazing—behold."

Matsuo Basho, untitled haiku

Gene Agress, Dave Kent, and Luong Le Dinh founded Berkeley Mills in 1988. Gene (now CEO) strives to create a company that reflects three core components: furniture that is well made, practices that are sensitive to the environment, and values that can be celebrated between employees, suppliers, and customers. These values, Gene believes, can be interchanged between the business side and the craft side. Adjectives such as honesty, integrity, and relationship building can be easily used for business or craft. Gene is sensitive to the fact that many individuals and companies are very good at creating excellent craft work, but many times those same principles do not carry over to the business side.

Gene was introduced to Asian design, art, and culture through his first wife, who was of Japanese ancestry. She taught him the subtleties of Japanese design and the power of simplicity in design. The technique of taking away the superfluous to reveal an inner beauty is seen in Gene's furniture designs.

Gene Agress (b. 1947). Photographer: Steve Burns.

The furniture piece that best embodies this infusion is Gene's interpretation of the Japanese tansu. Gene was one of the first people in America to design and construct this chest. The original Japanese tansus were a collection of stackable wooden boxes and cabinets. From his early stepped design he has developed a variety of pieces for the home office, A/V cabinets, and display cabinets, all based around the tansu aesthetic.

Gene has named the designs appropriately "East-West Furniture," calling the collection a "blend of design and structure, aesthetics and function." The furniture lines are a blend of Asian and American Arts & Crafts design.

Berkeley Mills is located in a 27,000 square foot showroom and workshop that sits in Berkeley, in the center of diverse Northern California. It is just minutes away from San Francisco, a short drive to Silicon Valley, and an easy trip to the famed wine

Photographer: Sean Sullivan.

The Arts & Crafts collection. Photographer: Sean Sullivan.

country of Sonoma and Napa Valleys. The showroom has large windows with a full view of the workshop. Believing that customers should be privy to the furniture making process, the building of furniture is in plain view of customers. The company employs 50 people, and is a sizeable operation.

The people of Berkeley Mills have invented innovative techniques and machinery to make the furniture making easier and more precise while keeping the integrity of each and every joint, frame, and finish. Some examples of their ingenuity are hydraulic tables that move up and down to suit the craftsperson's needs and the use of dry cleaning racks to hold all the different jigs. This frees up time for wood selection and detailing. Gene insists on premium grade hardwoods for even grain and

color, while making sure to purchase wood that is sustainably forested and harvested.

Gene considers himself a "constraints designer." When describing his designs, Gene says they are an extension of his clients' needs, "You have to ask the right questions and know construction."

Gene's love for his family was a determining factor in buying a decrepit craftsman bungalow just a block away from the showroom and workshop. With his wife, Diep, and three boys, Gene transformed the bungalow into a showpiece, complete with a Japanese garden and greenhouse. Diep has a passion for orchids and grows fantastically large blooms in their small greenhouse. Every Saturday she delivers huge bouquets to add a touch of home to the showroom.

Arts & Crafts sideboard. Wood: Honduras mahogany. Panels: shoji glass. Photographer: Don Tuttle.

Kaidan (step) tansu. Wood: cherry, birdseye maple drawer fronts. Photographer: Sean Sullivan.

Arts & Crafts armoire. Wood: Honduras mahogany, sapele pomele door fronts and panels. Photographer: Sean Sullivan.

Slatback bed, tansu blanket chest, and Arts & Crafts side table.Wood: cherry, maple, birdseye maple, ebony accents. Photographer: Sean Sullivan.

<u>Berkeley Mills</u>

Wave table, *Harp* chairs, *Kaidan* tansu. Wood: Cherry, birdseye maple, wenge. Chair seats: fabric. Photographer: Sean Sullivan.

Blackstone Design

"Texas always seemed so big, but you know you're in the largest state in the union when you're anchored down in Anchorage...Alaska."

Song by Michelle Shocked

Furniture making in Alaska has its own unique challenges and rewards. The terrain is rugged and uncompromising, materials are limited, and the weather can be frigid. But it is the natural beauty of Alaska with its vast wilderness and great potential for outdoor activities, that drew Mark Wedekind from his home state of Utah to the largest state in the union. That and the fact his wife Anne was offered a job promotion she couldn't pass up.

It was just after they had decided to stay in Utah, after traveling the desert southwest, that Anne got the offer to work as a staff photographer for the *Anchorage Daily News*. It was a chance of a lifetime. But with adventure comes trials and, to quote Mark, "I certainly don't live (here) for its proximity to a supply of hardwoods." There are some barriers to overcome. With only two wood suppliers, he has to make do or send for Appalachian hardwood, which is trucked to Seattle and then barged to Anchorage. He doesn't prefer this method because it prevents him from hand selecting each board.

Hand selecting boards is something he has enjoyed since he was a small child in Missouri. Mark can remember spending many days in the woods investigating the large hardwoods around his family's farm. He often retrieved logs from the firewood pile to turn into his creations, each time learning more about the grain and feel of the different species.

Mark Wedekind (b. 1963). Photographer: Anne Raup.

It was in Utah that Mark first began experimenting with making furniture. It came by way of necessity. "After college, five gallon buckets and milk crates became less acceptable as furniture," Mark jokes. They didn't have money to purchase new furniture and "there only seemed to be junk available," so Mark rose to the occasion.

Photographer: Anne Raup.

Detail of globe stand.
Photographer: Anne
Raup.

Globe stand. Wood: cherry. Photographer: Anne Raup.

Blackstone Design

After completing a house full of furniture his confidence and interest grew. Pouring his energy and time into furniture making, he soaked up books and magazines on the subject. He was striving to improve on his newfound techniques and began to experiment in different directions. Mark began to sell pieces to support his interest, enabling him to enhance his proficiency and develop his skills. "I'm no different now than when I first started. Every project gives me new ideas and I can't wait to use them. I'm always trying to find things to challenge me and push the limits."

Mark's creativity and motivation come from a wealth of sources. He finds inspiration in all mediums; a beautiful pot or a metal sculpture inspires Mark as much as a well designed and executed piece of furniture. Inspiration also comes from natural and organic forms, which the rich and varied landscape of Alaska provides. In fact, much of Mark and Anne's home is decorated from the landscape; rocks, pieces of driftwood, hornets nests all become objects d'art in their home.

The biggest obstacle of making and selling handcrafted furniture in Alaska has to do with the isolation. Mark doesn't get much interaction with other furniture makers because there are very few in Alaska. Promoting the work can be a familiar issue too, "I have the same challenge everyone who makes handcrafted furniture has: I have to educate people on the virtues of working with a small furniture shop."

"Furniture makers should make it a priority to design for everyday use and build pieces that will be appreciated for generations." Mark feels that "a living tree standing is a beautiful thing. If it is not going to stay as such, it should live on in beautiful objects."

Harp stand. Wood: maple, walnut. Top: leather panels.
Photographer: Anne Raup.

Screen. Wood: black walnut, cherry. Panels: woven painted silk by Pamela Lambe.
Photographer: Anne Raup.

Hinged detail of screen.
Photographer: Anne Raup.

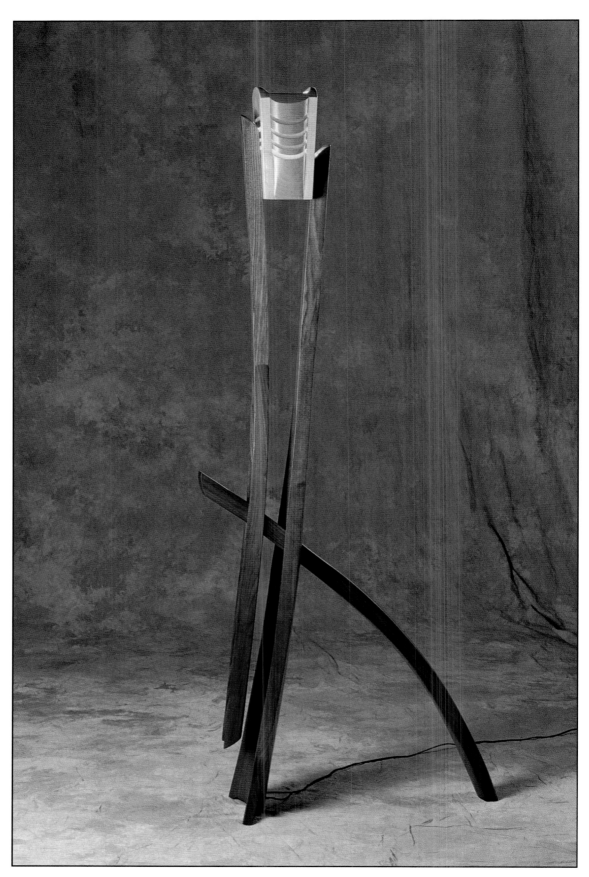

Floor lamp. Photographer: Anne Raup.

Brian M. Condran
Fine Woodworking

"One machine can do the work of fifty ordinary men, no machine can do the work of one extraordinary man."
Elbert Hubbard

Brian M. Condran (b. 1955). Photographer: Author.

Brian Condran says he isn't looking for a shocking reaction with his furniture. It's not art furniture where the main premise is "let's start a fight." Instead, he says, what makes his work special, "is the precision…the care of the grain." A student of James Krenov, he has developed his own graceful style, maintaining that it comes from discipline and knowledge.

His tenure at the College of Redwoods Fine Woodworking Program started as a summer session and ended up lasting two years. Surprisingly, the school's main focus is not design. He expected critiques and evaluations, but instead the school taught him "the hows and whys." Brian was taught a sensitivity that he did not think was possible.

For instance, in his tour de force, *Master's Watching*, a tribute to James Krenov and staff, he used 262 individual pieces of wood to create the inlaid image of James Krenov. Brian wanted to craft a cabinet that James would have made, but with a surprise. It is a reminder to Brian of the continuum of craft. James will always be watching as skills are passed on to other generations and the craft continues.

It has only been recently that Brian has become a woodworker. Before furniture making, he owned two auto parts stores for 15 years. He grew tired of dealing with surly customers and decided to return to school to learn more about architecture. One of his classes included half a semester devoted to designing and building furniture. He realized he liked making furniture more than architecture, so he made the switch.

Photographer: Seth Janofsky.

Master's Watching. Wood: acacia, European pear, holly, maple, boxwood, rosewood, walnut, ash, American cherry, teak, olive, beech, jatoba. Photographer: Kathleen Bellesiles.

Detail of *Master's Watching.*
Photographer: Kathleen Bellesiles.

Not knowing how or where to learn furniture making, he wasn't sure what to do next. Then good fortune stepped in. Brian's wife (Kathy) was working as an operating room nurse at the time and on one particular night she was the prep nurse. She walked into one of the patient rooms to take vitals and try to ease the woman's anxieties. As she asked the nervous patient about herself, the patient explained that she was an architect teaching at UC Berkeley. Kathy said that her husband liked architecture, but had decided he liked furniture making better. The architect said, "There is an old guy at a college up north who teaches furniture building and is pretty good." She went on to say that he had been around a long time and didn't know if he were still alive.

Kathy told Brian what she had learned, and Brian went straight to the placement office at his school and asked for every brochure about colleges north of San Francisco. Fortuitously he found the College of Redwoods out of the first handful he picked up. He drove up that following Saturday and was given the tour. Brian had found his calling; it was just meant to be.

Falling Leaf. Wood: American cherry, European beech, bocote, hickory, maple.
Photographer: Seth Janofsky.

Brian M. Condran Fine Woodworking

Beauty Within. Wood: cocobolo, granadillo, spalted English walnut, sucupira, bay laurel, lignum vitae, ebony, katalox, quilted maple, eastern maple, euro beech, olive. Photographer: Seth Janofsky.

<u>Brian M. Condran Fine Woodworking</u>

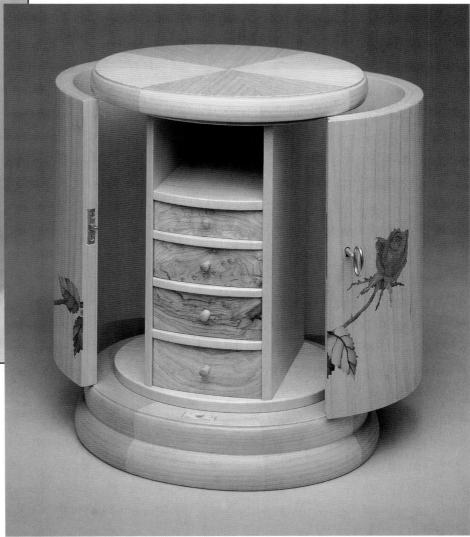

Dark Tower. Wood: granadillo, European pear, maple.
Photographer: Seth Janofsky.

Rose Case – open. Wood: Mendocino
cypress, pau marfin, African pink ivorywood,
bloodwood, poplar, lignum vitae, birdseye
maple, eastern maple, Swedish juniper.
Photographer: Kathleen Bellesiles.

Brian M. Condran Fine Woodworking

167

Victor DiNovi

"A sculptor is a person obsessed with the form and shape of things, and it's not just the shape of one thing, but the shape of anything and everything."
Henry Moore

Victor DiNovi (b. 1945) Photographer: Mark Singer.

Victor DiNovi is a man obsessed. Not only with the shape of things, but with creating something completely unexpected, yet functional. From his approach to furniture making to his construction techniques, he is unconventional. "Some furniture makers are too caught up in the process of making and the sanctity of the process," he explains. "What's important (to me) is the way the client reacts and people's reactions after I'm gone." Victor has been able to throw off the restraints that might encumber other woodworkers. He frowns upon traditional rectilinear forms that have historical overtones. Much like the famed architect Frank Gehry, Victor uses varied curvilinear forms to express function. One could say Victor is equal parts sculptor and woodworker.

His process runs contrary to traditional methods. Usually a woodworker will take lumber and then cut, sand, and fit the pieces together to produce the final work. Victor uses chunks of highly figured wood to make a rough form that resembles Legos stacked upon one another. Then he wears away the material with a handheld grinder, often using abrasive pads designed for auto bodywork. Occasionally, he will use a custom power chisel of sharpened steel mounted in an air hammer. Not only is he innovative with wood, but when necessity calls he can also fabricate a tool for his need.

There is a clear resemblance to nature in his pieces. Avoiding design books and woodworking magazines for fear that the visual images will be imprinted unconsciously on his brain, he turns to nature and his clients' tastes for his inspiration. Rarely producing a drawing, he prefers to create a prototype and then improvise when the time comes to actually craft the work. Choosing to improvise instead of plan because, he says, "my mechanics are innate, so I can focus on the design as I work."[1]

When asked what he finds most important in this process, he answers, "confidence." He explains, "Confidence

Photographer: Victor DiNovi.

Screen. Wood: Honduras mahogany. Panels: linen. Photographer: George Post.

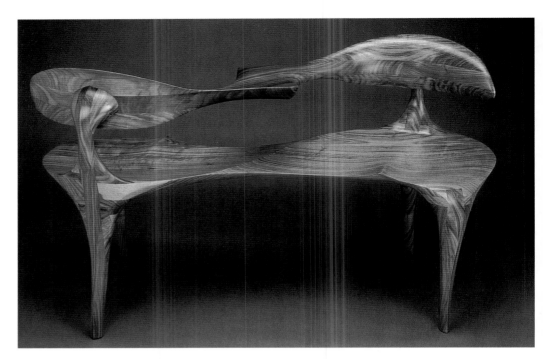

Tetatet. Wood: walnut.
Photographer: Victor DiNovi.

Globe stand. Wood: imbuia.
Photographer: Victor DiNovi.

makes it easy to stretch the envelope. Not being afraid to fail. If something doesn't work, you just make another one." It may be a bit easier for Victor, who comes from a family of artists and musicians. Originating from Brooklyn, New York, his father was a mural artist who would try any kind of work. Victor learned tenacity from his father because he would always find a way to do any project.

Victor feels the act of creation is as important as the object created. "Sometimes the 30 second inspiration that brought the design to your head is worth more than all the time you spent building it, because if you didn't have the inspiration, the other doesn't happen." Each piece, "gives me the confidence and the wherewithal to do the next one, and the next one is always the best one."

The May residence in Cabo San Lucas, Mexico. Wood: imbuia.
Photographer: Victor DiNovi.

Sideboard. Wood: teak. Photographer: Victor DiNovi.

Victor DiNovi

Outrigger canoe, Victor calls it "functional ocean sculpture." Wood: Philippine mahogany, koa. Additional materials: fiberglass and carbon fiber set in epoxy. Photographer: Victor DiNovi.

Schürch Woodwork

"Design in art is a recognition of the relation between various
things, various elements in the creative flux. You can't invent
a design. You recognize it, in the fourth dimension. That is,
with your blood and your bones, as well as with your eyes."
D.H. Lawrence

For craftsman and teacher Paul Schürch, leaving the States is how he gained experience and discovered his lifelong passion. At the age of 16 he traveled to Switzerland to learn how to build church organs and pianos. While there, he was introduced to veneering, and now, over 30 years later, he is one of America's leading marquetry experts.

In Switzerland his formal education consisted of mechanical engineering and aesthetical design in woodworking. He also sharpened his skills in working with wood, metal, leather, and fabric while considering how all these media play a role in creating musical instruments. While there he learned the importance of discipline and attention to detail, which have been major factors in shaping him into a fine craftsman.

His first trip to Europe would not be his last. He has returned many times and with each visit is rewarded with renewed creative energy and honed skills. On one of those trips he spent 1000 hours on a single piece of furniture, which involved keeping track of, sorting, handling, and assembling thousands of minute and fragile pieces. Concerning furniture design, he says, "Aesthetically, it is a balancing act where many aspects of design and diverse materials culminate into a vibrant work of art."[1] He now returns to Europe two to eight weeks per year to produce new projects involving wood and stone inlay.

In addition to wood and stone, Paul uses gems, shells, and metal to "take the art of marquetry beyond its former confines." He strives to be the best craftsman he can be, "no cutting corners, no compromises," maintaining that he constantly challenges himself to create works of art that will hopefully become the antiques of the future.

Like many craftspeople, he looks to nature for his furniture design, using the skills he learned in Europe to bring the elements of classically influenced styles, contemporary shapes, playful imagery, and exotic materials together in a balanced way. In this way, says Paul, he is

Paul Schürch (b. 1955). Photographer: Wayne McCall.

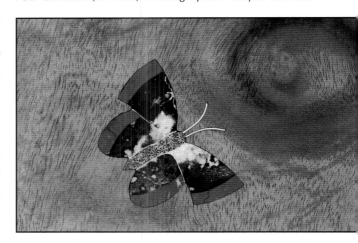

Photographer: Wayne McCall.

"creating a strong visual story that works in form, function, and aesthetics."

One way in which his furniture tells a story is in the "fair curve." Paul learned this technique on another visit to Europe when he studied traditional boat building in England. Fairing a curve is the ability to reproduce the curves found in nature. Paul describes these curves as graceful and pure, "without kinks, unnatural shapes, or

Shop chaos. Photographer: Wayne McCall.

flat spots."[2] He explains that you may not notice them, but when they are absent they are "surely missed." He says you may not see it with your eyes, but you will feel it in your heart.

It's true. Paul's pieces do have a powerful ability to impact you in the center of your being. It is the hours of labor that play out so effortlessly in each piece, drawing your eye, mind, and heart. Paul feels strongly about passing on this tradition to others. Today he teaches his techniques (some traditional Italian veneering and others he has invented) to any who are willing. He does this with videos, workshops, lectures, and apprenticeships.

Whether he is passing on his legacy through teaching or designing, it is the process that he finds most satisfying. Paul describes the task of rendering an idea into something moving and vibrant as an adventure. The reward, he says, is "immeasurable."

Schürch Woodwork

Cattail bed. Wood: maple frame, pollard ash, andiroba, tulipier, imbulia.
Stone: lapis lazule and marble. Metal: silver. Photographer: Wayne McCall.

Bamboo screen detail.
Photographer: Wayne McCall.

Bamboo screen. Wood: walnut frame, myrtle burl, poplar, tulipier, black pear.
Photographer: Wayne McCall.

Schürch Woodwork

Ribbon chest detail.
Photographer: Wayne McCall.

Ribbon chest. Wood: mahogany frame, Swiss steamed pear, satinwood, tulipwood, maple, black pear, walnut burl. Stone: lapis lazule. Photographer: Wayne McCall.

Schürch Woodwork

Thomas Stangeland
Artist/Craftsman

"Care more than others think wise. Risk more than others think safe. Dream more than others think practical. Expect more than others think possible."
Howard Shultz,
CEO of Starbucks Coffee

Seattle is probably best known for rain and coffee. But there is someone making quite a splash in this dreary town, and he doesn't have anything to do with the coffee or the weather. Thomas Stangeland has been crafting fine furniture for more than 15 years. Maybe that is why he is so easy to talk with and so readily able to articulate the intricacies of the furniture making process. Within the first few moments of a conversation, one knows that he would be a good teacher and a voracious learner.

At the age of ten Tom built intricate planes that would fly in excess of 100 mph. It was then, he says, that "the puzzle of building took hold and I was hooked for life." He moved to Seattle when he was 18, eventuallly graduating from the University of Washington with a B.A. in History. He worked his way through school as a chef at a popular Seattle restaurant (he maintains that there are many similarities between cooking and furniture making, namely starting with the best ingredients). Later, he took an odd job with famed artisan Emmet Day, and his love for building things was rekindled.

Tom finds resonance in the work of California architects Charles and Henry Greene. Using his own bungalow as a gauge, he tests the success of each new design by seeing how it fits. While he is also enamored with Art Deco furniture, Tom feels it doesn't harmonize in one's home as easily as the Arts & Crafts style. His commitment to craftsmanship and integrity is evident in all of his furniture.

Integrity plays a large part in Tom's life. When asked to build furniture for the guest house for Microsoft founder Bill Gates and his wife, Tom ended up having to decline.

Thomas Stangeland (b. 1960). Photographer: Mike Andeel

Photographer: Zach Flanders.

The guest house was the first building built on the Gates's property. It was to be a test building for the multimillion dollar complex, for studying the building materials and construction details. When Tom was shown the shop drawings for the chairs, he noticed that the

Anderson Server. Wood: Mahogany, ebony. Photographer: Greg Krogstad.

Wells bed. Wood: mahogany, ebony. Photographer: Richard McNamee.

Coffee table. Wood: mahogany. Top: fused glass. Photographer: Greg Krogstad.

<u>Thomas Stangeland Artist/Craftsman</u>

Madrona hutch. Wood: mahogany, ebony. Panels: glass. Metal: copper hardware.
Photographer: Greg Krogstad.

mortise and tenon connections would provide inadequate support. When he recommended that a new connection be designed while keeping the integrity of the piece, the designers gave Tom an emphatic "No." It was difficult, but he turned the job down.

Fortunately, many years later he won the commission to design and build furniture for the Disney Grand Hotel in Los Angeles, California. He submitted a pleasing design reminiscent of the Greene Brothers that caught the attention of the Disney officials. But it was Tom's superior finish that ultimately persuaded them. He recalls that in one of the meetings he was eating lunch at one of his own tables with the project manager. As Tom filled their glasses with water, the manager began to question the durability of the finish. Tom decided to demonstrate by pouring water on the table itself, until a pool surrounded the glass. As they ate their sandwiches, the puddle sat there "like a ringing phone going unanswered." The manger was about to crawl out of his skin, so Tom finally reached for the towel to wipe up the spill. The manager's only reply was, "You never told me you sold vacuum cleaners."

Tom is one of the founding members and owners of Northwest Fine Woodworking in Seattle, Washington. It is one of the largest handcrafted furniture co-op galleries in the country where the furniture makers all own a portion of the store. He continues to work and create new designs, maintaining that it is easy to stay in the shop when it rains all the time.

Thomas Stangeland Artist/Craftsman

Dining table and chairs. Wood: mahogany, ebony.
Metal: copper hardware. Chair seats: black leather.
Photographer: Greg Krogstad.

The Sevenfold Authority of the Holy Spirit in Craftsmanship

Photographer: Larry Hamill.

• Through the spirit of wisdom you know that created things proceed from God and that without Him nothing is.

• Through the spirit of understanding, you have received the capacity for practical knowledge of the order, the variety and the measure that you apply to your various kinds of work.

• Through the spirit of council you do not hide away the talent given you by God, but, working and teaching openly and with humility, you faithfully reveal it to those who desire to learn.

• Through the spirit of fortitude you shake off all the apathy of sloth, and whatever you commence with quick enthusiasm you carry through to completion with full vigor.

• Through the spirit of knowledge that is given to you, you are the master by virtue of your practical knowledge and you use in public the perfect abundance of your abounding heart with the confidence of a full mind.

• Through the spirit of piety you set a limit with pious consideration on what the work is to be, and for whom, as well as on the time, the amount, and the quality of work, and, lest the vice of greed or cupidity should steel in, on the amount or recompense.

• Through the spirit of the fear of the Lord you bear in mind that of yourself you are nothing able, and you ponder on the fact that you possess and desire nothing that is not given to you by God, but in faith, trust, and thankfulness, you ascribe to divine compassion whatever you know or are or can be.

The Divine Arts, by Theophilus
a tenth-century monk

The Furniture Makers

Mission Evolution
Arnold d'Epagnier
14201 Notley Rd.
Colesville, MD 20904
301.384.3201
www.missionevolution.com

Nojo Design
Jo Roessler
84 Cottage St.
Easthampton, MA 01027
413.527.9663
www.nojodesign.com

**Charles Shackleton Furniture
and Miranda Thomas Pottery**
Charles Shackleton
The Mill, Route 4, P.O. Box 43
Bridgewater, VT 05034
802.672.5175
www.shackletonthomas.com

Midwest

Raymond Bock Woodworking
Raymond Bock
E8380 County Road SS
Viroqua, WI 54665
608.637.8778

Doerr Woodworking
Michael Doerr
4371 Cty. Hwy. M
Sturgeon Bay, WI 54235
920.743.5631
www.michaeldoerr.com

G. Keener & Co.
Gary Keener
2936 Liberty Rd.
New Carlisle, OH 45344
937.846.1210
www.gkeenerco.com

Charles Radtke Furniture Maker
Charles Radtke
W62 N732 Riveredge Dr.
Cedarburg, WI 53012
262.375.8703
www.charlesradtke.com

Lorna Secrest
Casey Industrial Park
Pittsburgh, PA 15233
412.231.2296

South

Brian Boggs Chairmakers
Brian Boggs
118 Lester St.
Berea, KY 40403
859.986.4638
www.brianboggschairs.com

Michael Colca Furniture Maker
Michael Colca
711 Turtle Hill
Driftwood, TX 78619
800.972.5940
www.michaelcolca.com

Probst Furniture Makers
James Probst
Route 34
Hamlin, WV 25523
304.824.5916
www.probstfurniture.com

White Wind Woodworking
Daniel Kagay
777 Shady Lane #1
Austin, TX 78702
512.389.0099
www.danielkagay.com

West

Berkeley Mills
Gene Agress
2830 7th St.
Berkeley, CA 94710
510.549.2854
www.berkeleymills.com

Blackstone Design
Mark Wedekind
2136 Alder Dr.
Anchorage, AK 99508
907.279.4308
www.blackstonedesign.com

Brian M. Condran Fine Woodworking
Brian M. Condran
12 Dickson Lane
Martinez, CA 94553
925.372.8171

Victor DiNovi
925 C Calle Puerto Vallarta
Santa Barbara, CA 93103
805.962.3585

Schürch Woodwork
Paul Schürch
1324 Cacique St.
Santa Barbara, CA 93103
805.965.3821
www.schurchwoodwork.com

Thomas Stangeland, Artist/Craftsman
Thomas Stangeland
309 8th Ave. North
Seattle, WA 98109
206.622.2004
www.artistcraftsman.net

Endnotes

Chapter 1 The Simple Life

1. Wright, Frank Lloyd *The Natural House*. 1954. Reprint, New York, New York: Horizon Press, Inc. 1982, p. 188.

Chapter 6 James Krenov

1. Krenov, James. *A Cabinetmaker's Notebook.* New York, New York: Van Nostrand Reinhold Company, 1976, p. 109.
2. *Ibid.*, p. 118.
3. *Ibid.*, p. 15.

Chapter 7 Sam Maloof

1. Maloof, Sam. *Sam Maloof Woodworker.* Tokyo, Japan: Kodansha International Ltd., 1983. 187-188.
2. *Ibid.*, p. 64.

Chapter 8 Nakashima Woodworks

1. Nakashima, George. *The Soul of a Tree: A Woodworker's Reflections*. Tokyo, Japan: Kodansha International Ltd., 1981, p. 128.
2. Nakashima catalog.
3. *Ibid.*
4. Nakashima, George. *The Soul of a Tree: A Woodworker's Reflections*. Tokyo, Japan: Kodansha International Ltd., 1981. p. 70.
5. www.nakashimafoundation.org

Chapter 13 David B. Hellman and Associates

1. Volpe, Tod M., Beth Cathers and Alistair Duncan. *Treasures of the American Arts and Crafts Movement 1890-1920*. New York, New York: Harry N. Abrams, Inc., 1988, p. 6.

Chapter 18 Nojo Design

1. Home and Garden Television (HGTV) Modern Masters, Episode: MAS-705.

Chapter 23 Charles Radtke Furniture Maker

1. Reed, W. A. "Charles Radtke." *Porcupine* 2, No. 1 (Summer 1997), p. 52.
2. *Ibid.*, p. 52.
3. *Ibid.*, p. 52.
4. *Ibid.*, p. 49.
5. *Ibid.*, p. 51.
6. *Ibid.* p. 51.
7. *Ibid.* p. 51.
8. *Ibid.* p. 51.
9. *Ibid.* p. 53.

Chapter 32 Victor DiNovi

1. "Profile: Victor DiNovi" *Woodworker West* 10, No. 2 (March-April 1997) p. 56.

Chapter 33 Schürch Woodwork

1. Schürch, Paul. *Decorative Veneering with Master Craftsman Paul Schürch*. Santa Barbara, California: Wayne McCall & Associates, 2001, p. 6.
2. *Ibid*.

Bibliography

Books

Adamson, Jeremy. *The Furniture of Sam Maloof.* Washington D.C.: Smithsonian American Art Museum, W.W. Norton & Company, 2001.

Bowman, Leslie Greene. *American Arts & Crafts, Virtue in Design*. Boston, Massachusetts: Los Angeles County Museum of Art, Bulfinch Press/Little, Brown and Company, 1990.

Breen Pierce, Linda. *Choosing Simplicity.* Carmel, California: Gallagher Press, 2000.

Conway, Patricia. *Art for Everyday. The New Craft Movement.* New York, New York: Clarkson N. Potter, Inc., 1990.

Cooke, Edward S. Jr. *New American Furniture: The Second Generation of Studio Furnituremakers.* Boston, Massachusetts: Museum of Fine Arts, 1989.

Dooling, D.M. *A Way of Working, The Spiritual Dimension of Craft*. New York, New York: Parabola Books, 1979.

Ewald, Chase Reynolds. *Arts and Crafts Style and Spirit: Craftspeople of the Revival*. Salt Lake City, Utah: Gibbs Smith Publisher, 1999.

Furniture Society, The. *Furniture Studio: The Heart of the Functional Arts.* Edited by John Kelsey and Rick Mastelli. Free Union, Virginia: The Furniture Society, 1999.

_____. *Tradition in Contemporary Furniture.* Edited by Rick Mastelli and John Kelsey. Free Union, Virginia: The Furniture Society, 2001.

Gill, Eric. *A Holy Tradition of Woodworking*. West Stockbridge, Massachusetts: The Lindisfarne Press, Golgonooza Press, 1983.

Koren, Leonard. *Wabi Sabi, for Artists, Designers, Poets & Philosophers*. Berkeley, California: Stone Bridge Press, 1994.

Krenov, James. *A Cabinetmaker's Notebook.* New York, New York: Van Nostrand Reinhold Company, 1976.

_____. *The Fine Art of Cabinetmaking.* New York, New York: Van Nostrand Reinhold Company, 1977.

_____. *The Impractical Cabinetmaker.* New York, New York: Van Nostrand Reinhold Company, 1979.

_____. *James Krenov, Worker in Wood.* New York, New York: Van Nostrand Reinhold Company, 1981.

_____. *With Wakened Hands: Furniture by James Krenov and Students.* Fresno, California: Linden Publishing, Inc. Cambium Press, 2000.

Maloof, Sam. *Sam Maloof Woodworker.* Tokyo, Japan: Kodansha International Ltd., 1983.

Naisbitt, John. *Megatrends: Ten New Directions Transforming Our Lives*. New York, New York: Warner Books, Inc., 1982.

Naisbitt, John and Patricia Aburdene. *Megatrends 2000: Ten New Directions for the 1990's.* New York, New York: William Morrow and Company, 1990.

Naisbitt, John, with Nana Naisbitt and Douglas Philips. *High tech/high touch: Technology and Our Search for Meaning.* New York, New York: Broadway Books, 1999.

Pye, David. *The Nature and Art of Workmanship*. New York, New York: Cambridge University Press, 1968.

Stone, Michael. *Contemporary American Woodworkers.* Layton, Utah: Peregrine Smith Books, Gibbs M. Smith, Inc., 1986.

Yanagi, Sōetsu. *The Unknown Craftsman: A Japanese Insight to Beauty*. rev. ed. New York, New York: Kodansha International, 1989.

Magazines

Aibel, Robert. "Driving Ms. Mira" *The Modernism Magazine* 1, No. 2 (Fall 1998) 52-57.

Boggs, Brian. "The Evolution of a Chair." *Home Furniture* No. 8 (October 1996): 26-31.

_____. "A Chair Built for Comfort." *Home Furniture* No. 3 (Summer 1995): 76-78.

Chamber, Karen. "Tradition: From father to daughter, the Nakashima Style lives on." *American Style* (Winter 2000-2001): 54-63.

Fletcher, Rachel. "One With Wood." *Design Spirit* II, No. 2 (Summer 1990): 10-15.

Hinkel, Susan R. "A Maverick's Mansion." Art & Antiques (May 1988): 76-81.

Kuhl, Helen. "A Philosophy of Commitment." *Custom Woodworking Business* (February 2002): 63-66.

Miller, Charles. "Wharton Esherick's House and Studio." *Fine Homebuilding* No. 21 (June/July 1984) 35-43.

Reed, W. A. "Charles Radtke." *Porcupine* 2, No. 1 (Summer 1997) 46-59.

Newspapers

Killeen, Wendy. "Creative differences." *The Boston Globe*, Sunday, 25 April 1999, People & Places section, p. 13.

Schultz, Harriet. "Historic mill is setting for Cumberland furniture maker." *The (Maine) Forecaster*, 25 June 1998.

Bergengren, David. "Landmark Majestic Theater sold for furniture maker's business." *The (Springfield, Massachusetts) Union News*, 24 January 2001, Local section, p. 1b.

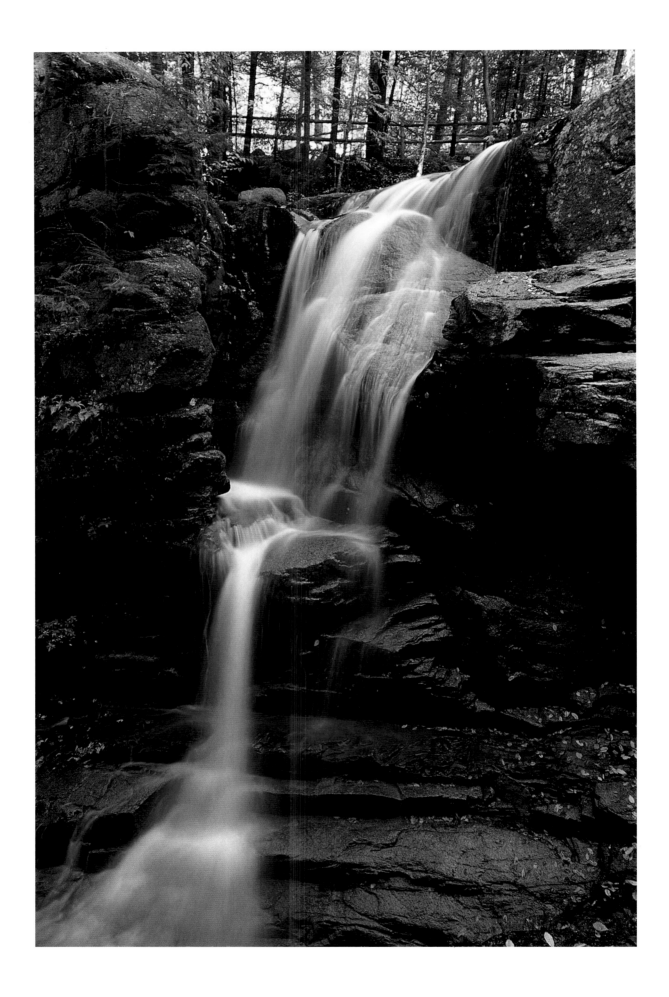